That Old-Time Religion in Modern America

THAT OLD-TIME RELIGION IN MODERN AMERICA

*Evangelical Protestantism
in the Twentieth Century*

D. G. Hart

The American Ways Series

IVAN R. DEE   *Chicago*

Library of Congress Cataloging-in-Publication Data:
Hart, D. G. (Darryl G.)
    That old-time religion in modern America : evangelical
  Protestantism in the twentieth century / D. G. Hart.
      p. cm. — (The American ways series)
    Includes bibliographical references (p.) and index.
    ISBN 1-56663-460-1 (cloth : alk. paper) — ISBN 1-56663-459-8
    (paper : alk. paper)
      1. Evangelicalism—United States—History—20th century. 2.
  United States—Church history—20th century. I. Title. II. Series.

BR1642.U5 H375 2002
280'.4'09730904—dc21   2002073763

Contents

Acknowledgments

EVERYTHING I KNOW about evangelicalism I learned in Sunday school. That is not entirely correct, but it may explain some of my ambivalence about evangelical Protestantism. Doubts about this form of Christianity aside, my understanding of and appreciation for the movement's innovative and entrepreneurial genius grew considerably during my tenure as director of the Institute for the Study of American Evangelicals at Wheaton College (Illinois). There my colleagues Mark A. Noll, Edith Blumhofer, and Larry Eskridge, along with the Institute's advisers, schooled me in the variety and potency of American evangelicalism. So when John Braeman invited me to write a book on twentieth-century evangelicalism in the United States, I felt obligated to do so if only to show I had learned something from my former office mates in Wheaton. Professor Braeman offered astute comments to an initial draft that tightened up my analysis. Ivan Dee did a wonderful job of tightening up my prose. To both of these men, and to my former colleagues, I express genuine thanks.

D. G. H.

Escondido, California
June 2002

That Old-Time Religion in Modern America

Introduction: Understanding Evangelicalism

The Big Kahuna may not have been a box office hit, but the 1999 movie starring Kevin Spacey and Danny DeVito offered a surprisingly candid glimpse of the way many Americans have come to regard the subject of this book, twentieth-century evangelicalism in the United States. The film features three men who work for an industrial lubricants firm and are assigned to host a cocktail party during a convention for industry-related vendors and producers. Two of the characters are experienced salesmen for whom the task of pitching the company's product has nurtured a degree of cynicism and weariness. The third character is a young, bright, and somewhat naive evangelical Protestant who works in the research division. The chief task of these three on this particular evening is to make contact with the "Big Kahuna," the owner of Indiana's largest manufacturing company, whose contract could salvage the salesmen's declining careers.

Over the course of the evening the evangelical identity of the young researcher, Bob, slowly emerges. Early in the movie Bob lets Phil (the character played by Danny DeVito), who is reading *Penthouse*, know that even looking lustfully at another woman is a sin. When Larry (the character played by Kevin Spacey) arrives, Bob (played by Peter Facinelli) declares once again that discussing sexual turn-ons is something he will not do because of his faith. He also informs his colleagues that he is not much of a drinker. Bob agrees to mix drinks during the party, but he has almost no knowledge of the ingredients in the most common cocktails.

Despite his lack of experience in the ways of traveling sales-men, Bob's evangelical identity does not become a source of antagonism until after the cocktail party, when Larry and Phil begin to attribute blame for letting the Big Kahuna get away. The ensuing discussion reveals that Mr. Fuller, whom the salesmen had at least hoped to meet, was actually present in the hospitality suite, though he had remained anonymous by wearing a different name tag. It also becomes clear that Bob had an extended conversation with him. As Larry and Phil push for details, Bob discloses that he not only talked to Mr. Fuller for a long time but also that they discussed *religion*, not industrial lubricants or even which lubricant Jesus himself would have used. When all seems lost, the salesmen send Bob to an after-hours party to which Mr. Fuller had invited him, and they give Bob simple and direct instructions about what to say.

Initially when Bob returns to the suite after several hours, things look good. He found the party and engaged Mr. Fuller in another long conversation. But instead of doing as Larry and Phil had asked, Bob reveals that he spent the whole time talking to the Big Kahuna about Christ and the forgiveness of sins. Larry is livid. He accuses Bob of having cheated the firm, doing the Lord's work on company time. Bob defends himself by arguing that religion is more important than business in the larger scheme, and he appeals to the Bible, especially the writings of the apostle Paul, to support his action. Tempers flare to the point where Bob and Larry wrestle briefly, with Phil having to pull his colleagues apart in order to break Bob's grip around Larry's neck.

Although this brief description of *The Big Kahuna* may portray Bob, the evangelical, as a believer who is self-righteous and judgmental, the movie actually depicts him as a genuinely warm, honorable, and decent young man. He may be naive, but he is clearly likable. Bob, for instance, enjoys the company of his non-Christian colleagues, even if he doesn't approve of the way they live their lives. He may be gullible about business matters, but his innocence appears to be the result of youth more than faith. And even though he botches the assignment to network with Mr. Fuller, Bob remains an amiable fellow with whom most viewers would feel comfortable sharing a meal (as long as it did not involve heavy drinking). In this respect *The Big Kahuna* was a breakthrough film for evangelicals on the big screen. In the past, Hollywood movies in which evangelicals played prominent roles usually involved charlatan preachers, such as *Elmer Gantry* (1960) or *The Apostle* (1997), or born-again Protestants doing their best to block the advance of reason, such as *Inherit the Wind* (1960). In his review of *The Big Kahuna*, Roger Ebert faulted film critics for neglecting religion. "You can search the reviews in vain for any mention of Jesus Christ," he writes. "Most of the reviewers seem to have forgotten that Bob is born again." Bob had the Big Kahuna "in the palm of his hand and blew the deal" because of his faith.

Whatever *The Big Kahuna* and its reception may reveal about Hollywood and those assigned to comment on its wares, even more important is the film's remarkably accurate depiction of an ordinary evangelical. This category describes roughly twenty million Americans, or about 7 percent of the population. On the one hand, as this movie reveals, evangelicals are out of place in modern American society. As a born-again Protestant, Bob marches to the beat of a different drummer, a beat supplied not by capital gains or identity politics but by the Bible and an interest in converting others. On the other hand, the average evangelical is thoroughly assimilated to American ways of life. Bob is not odd like the Amish, for example, who have self-consciously, on the basis of religious ideals, chosen an agrarian way of life very different from the way most Americans live. In fact, evangelicals are so well adapted to American norms that, as Bob's character also demonstrates, the only way to tell they are different is when they talk about Christ or the Bible, or when they refrain from alcohol or sexual innuendo.

This book is about twentieth-century evangelicalism and, specifically, the tension between born-again Protestantism's simultaneous conformity to and discomfort with American ways. It begins with the premise that evangelicalism is the most American version of Christianity, and covers the period beginning in the 1920s when evangelicalism gained a reputation for being out of synch with mainstream American thought and culture. Because most of this book examines the oddness of twentieth-century evangelicalism against the backdrop of American culture, a few words need to be offered at the outset about born-again Protestant history before the twentieth-century, a time when evangelicalism emerged as a quintessentially American faith.

The roots of evangelical Protestantism go back to the religious fervor of British Protestants in colonial North America. That fervor prompted a revival commonly referred to as the First Great Awakening. Its leaders were Jonathan Edwards (1703–1758), a remarkably gifted theologian and philosopher who pastored a church in Northhampton, Massachusetts, and George Whitefield (1715–1770), an Anglican priest who came to the colonies in 1739 to raise funding for a new orphanage in Georgia. A first-rate thinker, Edwards supplied the rationale for the new Protestantism that was emerging in the 1730s and 1740s, while Whitefield functioned as the model of evangelicalism in the way he preached and promoted the awakening. Together the two men sought to shake new life into the churches that they believed were too formal and lifeless.

Before the First Great Awakening, churches in colonial America took their lead from European Protestantism, with a learned clergy and the formalities of liturgy and church polity informing Protestant faith and practice in the New World. Ministers needed formal training in order to be ordained; their sermons were supposed to reflect that learning, and the services they conducted were designed to immerse church members in the beliefs and ceremonies that religious authorities had prescribed. This kind of Protestantism, whether Episcopalian, Lutheran, Presbyterian, Reformed, or Congregationalist—the main branches of the Reformation—stressed faith as a lifelong struggle with sin and temptation, for which the teaching of and worship in the church provided assistance and encouragement. This older version of Protestantism was objective (rather than personal) in the sense that to be a church member involved being conformed to the doctrines and liturgy of the church. And it was corporate in the sense that by participating in the worship of the church, Christians lost some of their individual identity and became part of a community of believers united by the teaching and ministry of the church.

The revivals led by Edwards and Whitefield planted seeds that would challenge this older version of Protestantism and eventually yield the basic ingredients of evangelicalism. Of foremost importance to this religious awakening was the experience of conversion. Evangelical ministers broke with the established pattern of learned sermons and began to preach in ways designed to bring hearers to a point of crisis, at which they despaired over their sinfulness and experienced the love of God in an immediate way. Whitefield pioneered this new form of preaching, expressing the truths of Christianity in the colloquial language of everyday life. Edwards wrote eloquently in defense of conversion as the only sufficient basis for authentic faith. But evangelical religion did not stop with the born-again experience. It also included holy living. The leading revivalists expected converts to show dramatically the difference that religion made in their lives by behaving in a visibly devout manner, whether by abstaining from certain worldly activities or by performing righteous deeds. In other words, conversion was such a profound experience that it would be clearly evident in the lives of converts. To be sure, precedents existed both within English and German Protestantism for the emerging evangelical way of faith. But the revivals of the 1730s and 1740s proved so dramatic and powerful that evangelicalism emerged as virtually a new form of Protestantism, one centered in the experience and affairs of the individual believer as opposed to the teaching and worship of the church.

Evangelicalism's stress upon personal experience and the individual's good works had important repercussions for the established churches and clergy. First, it demanded that all ministers promote the awakening. If they did not, their devotion to Christianity could easily be questioned. Second, it undermined traditional forms of church life and ministry by making experience and good behavior the most important matters for true believers. If the teaching and worship of the established churches were not producing conversions, they were examples of nominal Christianity where believers and clergy were simply going through the motions. At the same time, the emphasis on holy living taught that what happened in converts' lives during the course of the week was just as vital as, if not more important than, the activities of the church on Sunday. And by raising questions about the effectiveness of the older forms of Protestantism and the clergy who administered them, evangelicalism's new form of devotion ended up freeing the laity to take control of their religious lives. No longer did Protestant believers need to rely upon the teaching and advice of church officers; by encountering firsthand the presence and peace of God, converts were free to read the Bible for themselves without having to rely upon the interpretations of church officers or the creeds of their churches. Protestantism since the Reformation has indeed stressed the Bible as the sole authority in religious matters, in contrast to church tradition and clergy, and thus has cultivated the practice of Bible reading by laity and clergy alike. But the established Protestant churches also insisted that clergy possessed legitimate authority to teach and govern the affairs of the church. Evangelicalism threw this governance into question.

Some discussions of evangelicalism yield so many different definitions that keeping track of the various historical twists and theological nuances requires a glossary of key terms. For instance, distinctions are often made among evangelicals, fundamentalists, Pentecostals, Wesleyans, and charismatics. All of these groups qualify as evangelical in some sense, the argument runs, but they also have distinct tendencies or peculiar practices. For the purpose of this book, evangelicalism is simply this modified form of Protestantism that emerged in eighteenth-century colonial America among white settlers and continues down to the present. It is a form of devotion that, by making conversion and holiness central, challenged the established and churchly practices of European Protestantism.* In this sense, distinctions among various strains of evangelicalism lose sight of this central point, namely, that any Protestant who emphasizes the subjective and ethical aspects of Christianity, rather than its official and churchly characteristics, is an evangelical. That is, evangelicalism is essentially a low-

---

*This book does not address the experience of African Americans who are evangelicals. One reason is that contemporary African Americans, Protestants included, are for good or ill known more for their race than their religion, unlike white evangelicals who are identified more by their religion than their ethnicity. The other reason is that this book synthesizes recent scholarship on American evangelicals, a body of work that has yet to incorporate successfully the experience of African-American evangelicals into the main narrative.

church expression of Protestantism, because what matters most to born-again Protestants is what occurs not inside the church but in their own personal affairs. Simply put, evangelicalism is synonymous with born-again Protestantism because evangelicals stake the authenticity of Christian faith upon the conversion experience, not church membership.

Evangelicalism emerged from the First Great Awakening well prepared to become the popular religious idiom of the United States before the twentieth century. This status was due not only to the accomplishments of Whitefield and Edwards but also to crucial developments in the life of the new nation. The defining moment in the life of the United States was the War for Independence and the subsequent formation of a new and sovereign nation. The American Revolution had far-reaching implications for religion. First off, the United States was founded as an enlightened country, that is, as a society based upon human powers of reasoning as opposed to such traditional authorities as the monarchy and church. When the Declaration of Independence stated, "We hold these truths to be self-evident . . . ," it reflected a concerted effort on the part of the Founding Fathers to let reason rather than revelation, land, or blood determine the nature of good government and an orderly society.

In Europe, as in the case of the French Revolution, Enlightenment philosophy often nurtured hostility to the church and to orthodox Christianity. In the United States, however, religion appeared to be on the side of revolution, and evangelicalism deserved a good deal of credit for this perception. On the one hand, many evangelicals in the Presbyterian, Reformed, Congregationalist, and Baptist denominations had already—during the First Great Awakening—transformed their suspicion of clergy and established churches into an opposition to the British monarch and the Church of England. On the other hand, evangelical Protestantism overlapped with Enlightenment conceptions of knowledge in two ways. First, by demanding visible evidence of conversion for faith to be genuine, evangelicals were arguing in the religious sphere for a similar kind of proof that Enlightenment scientists required for understanding nature or society. Second, by assuming that ordinary Christians could understand the Bible as well the learned, evangelicals embraced the democratic understanding of reason inherent in the Enlightenment. As such, born-again Protestantism was not at odds but in harmony with the ideals that inspired the founding of the Republic. Of course, the skeptical side of the Enlightenment, most evident in France and found in American figures such as Thomas Paine, prompted evangelicals to oppose aspects of the new learning when it exalted reason over revelation. Consequently evangelical Protestantism was not always compatible with the Enlightenment. But it was much more congenial than older interpretations allow, thanks to evangelicals' own understanding of religious truth and the way individuals appropriate it.

Evangelicalism not only supported America's political philosophy, it benefited directly from the way the Founding Fathers resolved questions about the place of religion in the new nation. By prohibiting congressional support for an established church, the First Amendment to the United States Constitution in effect made belief voluntary. Churches could not depend on the government for tax subsidies (though some did at the state level) and so were forced to find their own support by attracting adherents. Religious disestablishment played directly into the hands of those denominations, such as Baptist and Methodist, who were the greatest proponents of evangelicalism's anti-formal and nonliturgical version of Protestantism. Indeed, the fastest-growing churches in the first half of the nineteenth century were those denominations freed from relying upon clergy and the trappings that often came with the ordained ministry. Evangelicalism encouraged the laity to take greater control of their religious lives through their own study and forms of devotion. As such, rather than finding the disestablishment of religion to be a curse, evangelical Protestants actually benefited, at least during the nineteenth century, from a voluntary system of church affiliation.

The second important development for evangelicalism during the nineteenth century was the outcome of the political struggles that resulted in the Civil War. From 1800 to 1860, as Americans attempted to forge a virtuous and orderly society independent from traditional European authorities, evangelicalism became what one historian has called "the functional equivalent of an established church." It did so largely from momentum supplied by the Second Great Awakening, a series of revivals surging during the 1820s and 1830s. In many respects these were similar to those of the eighteenth century but with even greater social consequences. Born-again Protestants launched a series of social reforms based on the evangelical premise that conversion leads to righteous lives and holy societies. They formed associations whose purpose was to eliminate every kind of evil. In the North this involved opposition to slavery, Sabbath-breaking, and alcohol, and an effort to provide care and education for those in need. Many of the Protestants who supported and worked for this "Benevolent Empire" were also active in politics, joining first the Whig party and later helping to found the Republican party. Evangelicalism was thus the religious complement to a political and social outlook that sought to make the United States a large, efficient, and unified nation, not a collection of various locales with different identities. This was the same perspective that rallied the North during the Civil War to fight for the Union rather than allowing the South to secede, and to combat slavery's violation of a person's right to choose his or her own way in the world. Obviously the South's economic and political arrangements prevented Southern evangelicals from mimicking their religious peers in the North. But although born-again Protestantism south of the Mason-Dixon Line came out on a different side in the debates over slavery and Union, and lacked the organizational muscle of Northern evangelicalism, it nevertheless shared the same zeal for holy living to be worked out in visible ways that implicitly involved the establishment of a godly society.

The support that evangelicalism supplied in creating an American identity involved more than politics. Before the 1920s (some would say the 1960s), American culture was chiefly the product of Anglo-American Protestants, a group that sociologists have named WASP (White Anglo-Saxon Protestants). In 1892, for instance, when the justices of the Supreme Court described the religious identity of the United States, they did so in the following terms:

> If we pass beyond these matters to a view of American life as expressed by its laws, its business, its customs, and its society, we find everywhere a clear recognition of the same truth. Among other matters note the following: The form of oath universally prevailing, concluding with an appeal to the Almighty; the custom of opening sessions of all deliberative bodies and most conventions with prayer; the prefatory words of all wills, "In the name of God, Amen"; the laws respecting the observance of the Sabbath, with the general cessation of all secular business, and the closing of courts, legislatures, and other similar public assemblies on that day; ... These, and many other matters which might be noticed, add a volume of unofficial declarations to the mass of organic utterances that this is a Christian nation.

This understanding of American culture helps explain the comments of foreign observers who were regularly struck by the United States' high degree of religiosity. Lord James Bryce, a British visitor in the late nineteenth century, observed in *The American Commonwealth* (1891), "The whole matter may, I think, be summed up by saying that Christianity is in fact to be understood, though not the legally established religion, yet the national religion." Americans, he added, "deem the general acceptance of Christianity to be one of the main sources of their national prosperity, and their nation a special object of Divine favor." If readers of Bryce's book wondered about the Christianity of which he wrote, André Siegfried, a French visitor writing almost four decades later, asserted emphatically in *America Comes of Age* (1927), "No one can possibly understand the United States without a profound, almost innate appreciation of their Puritanism." Although Siegfried may not have understood all the nuances of English-speaking Protestantism, his treatment of "Puritanism" indicated that the faith he had in mind was the evangelical one that had shaped the nation's "outlook on moral problems."

Few historians would dispute the impact of evangelicalism on the United States during the century after the nation's founding. But the nature of evangelical Protestantism's influence has not always been sufficiently appreciated. What made born-again Protestantism successful in its penetration of American culture was its independence from such traditional structures of historic Christianity as church officers, official creeds, and formal liturgies. Had evangelical leaders needed to rely upon training clergy, constructing church buildings, and circulating the same hymnals or books of prayer, the scope of their influence would likely have been significantly diminished. But the main point of born-again Protestantism was that the formalities of official Protestantism were not as important as the average Christian's daily experience. Evangelical Protestantism was and continued to be above all a relevant faith that informed all walks of life. As such, it could not be confined to the official activities of a specific church; it extended wherever its adherents took it. Because of evangelicalism's inherent informality, along with the zeal it inspired for transforming every realm of life according to biblical truth, this form of Protestantism had nowhere to go except outside the churches and into American society. In other words, evangelicalism freed Protestants to put their energies into the creation of a society that reflected Christian mores.

On any number of fronts, evangelicalism entered the period after the North's victory at Appomattox as the religion most in harmony with American norms and history. Although the late nineteenth and early twentieth centuries would witness challenges to evangelical influence, throughout the twentieth century born-again Protestants have been unable to forget their former position of importance in the United States. Consequently they have awkwardly worn the oddness that others see in them. For evangelicals, if anything is odd about evangelicalism in the United States it is that American society has turned its back on the faith that had helped form a great nation. They believe the Bobs of the world, like the young associate in *The Big Kahuna*, are the normal ones, not the Larrys and Phils, who think Bob strange because of his faith.

Unfortunately for contemporary evangelicals living in the United States, they are the ones who don't seem to fit in. This is not simply the perception of nonevangelicals but also the conclusion of born-again Protestants themselves. A recent sociological study of contemporary evangelicalism, for instance, revealed that born-again Protestants feel out of place in American society. Part of this owes to the evangelical sense that America was their homeland and now has rejected the faith of their parents and grandparents. One of the evangelical men interviewed for this study commented:

America was founded on Christian principles. Some of our founding fathers were maybe immoral in some of their lifestyles, but they as a whole founded our nation on "one nation under God." They believed in a supreme being, in God Almighty, and they wanted our nation to espouse those values and beliefs. . . . Today it's shaky. Our nation is on the edge and falling from the true meaning of being a Christian nation. I think its foundation is being eroded from way down deep.

An evangelical woman from a different denomination agreed with this gloomy assessment of America's spiritual climate. "There used to be higher family values," she commented, "higher morals, whereas today, you know, anything goes!" Statements like these reveal the degree to which evangelical Protestants feel out of sorts. Their unease stems directly from the perceived antagonism between their own religious convictions and those of the surrounding society.

These perceptions are not simply the product of evangelical paranoia. A number of born-again Protestants interviewed in this study identified objective criteria by which American social and cultural institutions greet their beliefs with hostility and derision. One woman complained about the media's stereotypes of evangelicals "as not having much intellectual capacity." Another female evangelical lamented the insensitivity of public school officials. The schools, she declared, "have completely removed anything that has to do with Christianity or the Bible or any of that" but will tolerate "books like *Heather Has Two Mommies*, real secular and anti-moral books." When Christian holidays come around, according to another evangelical woman, "you can't have any mention of what it is about. But you can celebrate Halloween." To her, the public schools' avoidance of Christian themes or teaching feels like "discrimination." To another evangelical man interviewed, this hostility is entirely predictable given what the Bible teaches about the differences between believers and nonbelievers. He explained:

There are two opposing views, a Christian worldview and a secular worldview. And one is going to be crowded out and denied their freedom to live by the standards they hold to. They might say "well just leave us alone," but the thing is they won't leave the Christian community alone. They are impinging on us. There is a war going on, and when you're in a warfare, you battle to take ground, not just hold it. They're not just trying to hold ground, they are trying to take ground, which is our right to live in a Christian society.

Nevertheless the hostility that evangelicals feel from the surrounding culture is not theirs alone. The sociologists who conducted this survey also included nonevangelical Americans, and their responses indicated that the antagonism sensed by evangelicals was prompted in part by the opposition that born-again Protestants themselves manifested toward American ways. According to one Lutheran man:

I think evangelical can have a negative connotation, it really can. That you're gonna be out there, you know, pointing your finger and saying, "If you don't believe the way I believe, you're in big trouble." I think we have to be real careful about judging other people's spiritual beliefs. . . . So I don't want to be labeled an evangelical, period. I don't want that to be what people say about me.

Negative impressions like this one were partly the result of evangelical efforts in proselytizing, which for approximately half of those surveyed turned out to be a "negative experience." Evangelicals also alienated other Americans through their efforts to influence public issues. Another Lutheran man indicated that evangelical fears about gay rights or New Age religions were "unfounded paranoia," little more than "rationalizations to meet their self-serving interests." Responses such as these led Christian Smith, a sociologist at the University of North Carolina who directed the survey, to conclude that evangelicals face "a serious public relations problem." He writes:

> Evangelicals may believe in the practical moral superiority of their particular Christian way of life. But most other Americans apparently do not see it that way. Evangelicals may think they have real solutions to offer the world for its problems. But few Americans who are not conservative Protestants see the kinds of solutions that evangelicals are offering as attractive or helpful.

But these results were not the worst news for evangelicals. The nonevangelicals he surveyed, according to Smith, indicated that "it was generally not what evangelicals might admit are their worst qualities, but rather what they view as their best features that most alienated outsiders." For this reason, Smith suggests that there is little evangelicals can do to change their image as cultural outsiders in the United States.

The central theme in the pages that follow is the reversal of evangelical fortunes over the course of the twentieth century. How did born-again Protestants, who were by most accounts among the most respected Americans, become in the minds of many at best an annoyance and at worst a threat to civil society? To be sure, evangelicals are not solely responsible for this dramatic change in perceptions. The United States is a very different place in 2000 than it was in 1900. Still, the emphasis in this survey of twentieth-century American evangelicalism will be on the internal dynamics of this religious movement and the factors that have contributed to born-again Protestantism's current awkward relationship with American culture and society.

The experience of evangelical Protestants in twentieth-century America falls roughly into three periods. The first begins a few decades before 1900 and continues until 1920. During this time those Protestants with convictions and practices that today would be called evangelical were indistinguishable from "mainline" or "liberal" Protestants. In other words, evangelical and mainline Protestantism had yet to emerge as distinct categories with separate denominations, organizations, and personalities. Although differences between liberal and evangelical segments of the largest Protestant churches were beginning to surface, most members of these denominations considered themselves evangelical in the sense that they affirmed the deity of Christ, the authority of the Bible, the necessity of conversion, and the duty of holy living. At the same time evangelical Protestantism of this kind was the most influential of America's religions. Its establishment may not have been official, but its ideals and practices informed American public life in palpable ways.

This pattern changed dramatically during the 1920s. This was the decade when the fundamentalist-modernist controversy erupted and proved to be crucial to the creation of evangelical Protestantism as most Americans now know it. During the ecclesiastical and cultural contests of the 1920s, the issues that had begun to trouble Protestants from the 1880s on finally came to a head. Fundamentalists—the party from which modern evangelicalism would emerge—opposed the attempt by liberal Protestants to accommodate Christianity to modern American culture. They insisted, contrary to liberal thought, that Christianity demanded renunciation of the world. The task of all believers was to save sinners from worldliness and demonstrate biblical holiness. From the fundamentalists' perspective, the liberal effort to redeem society through the Social Gospel, that is, by applying the ideals of Jesus to political and economic life, represented a break with the true evangelical tradition of reforming society through changed lives (that is, individual conversion). Because fundamentalists lost these arguments, and because of their opposition to the decadence of American society, they adopted a separatist outlook that prompted the formation of a religious subculture in which they could preserve the old-time evangelical religion as they understood it.

The fundamentalists' momentous decision to establish new institutions for propagating the Christian religion would have important repercussions for evangelical self-understanding. By breaking from the structures of the largest Protestant denominations, fundamentalists and their evangelical successors lost contact with many of the religious and cultural precedents established by nineteenth-century evangelicals. In effect, twentieth-century evangelicals think about their faith and America in terms very similar to those used by a previous generation, but they were forced to act very differently. They had to create new structures from scratch amidst the new circumstances confronting them in twentieth-century America—big government, big business, and a much more diverse culture.

The controversies of the 1920s were thus important for the emergence of evangelicalism in its modern sense, a movement at odds with the direction of American society. Yet as isolated as fundamentalists became during the two decades after the 1920s, their retrenchment paid the dividend of establishing a distinct religious identity. After the 1940s, an evangelical was someone who may have believed and practiced the same religion as nineteenth-century Protestants—a high regard for the Bible and its practicality, belief in the necessity of conversion and holy living, and zeal in seeking the conversion of others. But this form of faith no longer prevailed in America's oldest and largest denominations and their affiliated organizations. Instead evangelicalism spawned its own institutions, independent from the older Protestant churches. To be evangelical was, in effect, to be a Protestant distinct from the mainline.

The last period of evangelical Protestantism begins with

the 1960s, when evangelicals gradually emerged from their religious ghetto into positions of visibility and influence. They did so most notably in the political sphere by taking an active role in promoting family values and supporting election candidates with the proper moral convictions. But evangelicals also began to enter other arenas of American society, from higher education to popular culture. In so doing, evangelicalism began to recover some of the luster it had shown during the nineteenth century when it influenced the development of the United States in profound ways. And yet the society in which evangelicals began to reassert themselves was significantly different from the one on which their spiritual ancestors had left their mark. The difference between the relatively homogeneous culture of nineteenth-century America and the multicultural United States of the late twentieth century has been at the heart of evangelicals' sense of alienation from the secular media, public education, and American politics. Aspiring to recover America's moral and spiritual direction, evangelicals find themselves unwanted, expendable, and in some cases a nuisance. This is exactly the opposite of what their beliefs and their history in the United States tell them, namely, that the greatness of the United States depends upon the virtue and therefore the faith of its citizens.

This tension between evangelicals' perception of their own importance to American society, and the difficulty of granting any single religion that kind of importance in a society as diverse as the United States, is at the heart of the story that follows. Evangelical religion teaches its adherents that Christianity is the most important reality of human life, so much so that other considerations pale in comparison. The reality of secular America, however, is that its citizens need to find values other than religious faith to achieve a common purpose. The difference between the demands of evangelicalism and of secular society is exactly what Bob, the evangelical character in *The Big Kahuna*, experienced when he evangelized instead of joining Larry and Phil in selling their firm's product. How evangelicals like Bob decided to follow their beliefs rather than the instructions of society is what the following pages attempt to explain.

PART ONE

An Evangelical Ghetto
in WASP America, 1920–1960

1

A Peculiar People, a Divine Book

DAYTON, TENNESSEE, was an unlikely setting for what many regarded as the "Trial of the Century." A small country town of roughly eighteen hundred in 1925, stimulated briefly during the 1890s by ties to Northern rail lines, Dayton was hardly the sort of place where one would have expected the reason of scientists to tangle with the biblical faith of middle America. New York City or Chicago would have been more likely sites for a showdown between dogma and science. Yet the reporters and lawyers who descended upon this out-of-the-way town in the summer of 1925, for the trial of John T. Scopes for teaching evolution in the local high school, ended up witnessing the single most important event in the history of evangelical Protestantism in the United States.

At the most basic level, the Scopes Trial was a straightforward matter. In 1925, following the lead of other Southern states such as Florida and Kentucky, Tennessee legislators passed a law that prohibited the teaching in public schools "of any theory that denies the story of the Divine Creation of man as taught in the Bible." Scopes, who taught math and physics and coached football at the Rhea County high school, also used a biology textbook that clearly taught evolution. The jury's verdict which found Scopes guilty was not a surprise. What was amazing was how a clear-cut violation of state law turned into a trial of evangelical Protestantism. Scopes himself was a pawn in a larger scheme by Dayton civic boosters and secular elites to generate publicity for the town and expose the backwardness of evangelicals' literal interpretations of the Bible. As Clarence Darrow, the prominent attorney for the defense, said in his closing statement at the trial, "We have done our best to turn the tide . . . of testing every fact in science by a religious doctrine." William Jennings Bryan, a life-long leader in the Democratic party and chief prosecutor in the Scopes Trial, took Darrow's bait and declared his intention "to protect the word of God against the greatest atheist or agnostic in the United States." Such rhetoric demonstrated how a simple state law and the trial it provoked became a public spectacle that pitted the progressive views of science against the backward ideas of the Bible.

Although the Bible had long been a symbol of the United States' political and cultural superiority, the Scopes Trial severed the link between biblical religion and America's progress. This was ironic both because evolution lost in the trial and because William Jennings Bryan in many ways embodied the close connection between the Bible's values and American ideals of freedom, equality, and democracy. A three-time Democratic nominee for president (1896, 1900, and 1908), Bryan was part of a generation of American politicians who asserted that Christianity provided light on the path toward moral and cultural improvement, both in the United States and around the world. By the late 1920s, however, such a positive estimate of the Bible was harder to make without serious qualification. The Bible would continue to inform discussions about American society after the 1920s, but those conversations would not include Bible believers of the kind who shared Bryan's evangelical faith. And the reason had everything to do with Americans' high estimate of science and the progress it promised. If belief in the Bible involved questioning science, as testimony at the Scopes Trial clearly indicated, biblical faith would have to be modified. While the leadership of the mainline Protestant churches continued to revise their convictions in the light of scientific discovery, evangelicals read the Bible and drew ideas from it that forced born-again Bible believers into cultural isolation.

The Bible had functioned during nineteenth-century American history as an icon of moral authority and common decency, as is clearly illustrated by the way it was employed by public leaders and in public institutions. When Grover Cleveland (1837–1908), the twenty-second and twenty-fourth president of the United States, said, "The Bible is good enough for me: just the old book under which I was brought up," he was expressing a sentiment shared by many Americans and fellow politicians. And these were not simply the convictions of zealous church members. Abraham Lincoln (1809–1865), the sixteenth president, admitted that he was not a member of a Christian church, but this did not mean he had ever "denied the truth of the Scriptures." Lincoln's reliance on biblical imagery was unmistakable in one of his most memorable speeches, the Second Inaugural Address, where he spoke of the inscrutability of God's providence, quoted the Bible—"the judgments of the Lord are just and true"—and then bent down and kissed the Bible on which he had placed his hand while taking oaths as the nation's chief executive. So firm was the Bible's grip on American culture that even one of the book's greatest skeptics, Thomas Jefferson (1743–1826), the third president and proponent of enlightened reason over dogmatic faith, could not help producing his own version of the Christian scriptures. In Jefferson's Bible, the "unreasonable" parts from the Old Testament and many of the New Testament's epistles were omitted, but the parts of the Gospels that contained Christ's sound ethical teaching and example remained intact.

American presidents did not merely pay lip service to the Bible but oversaw and in some cases heartily approved of the book's introduction into public life. One such example came from the sphere of public schooling. The practice of Bible reading and prayer in public schools has a long history in the United States that goes back to the practices of the American colonists. In the middle decades of the nineteenth century, the custom became law as state legislatures required Bible reading as a way of promoting religion and virtuous attitudes and behavior among students. Without religion, most Americans believed, the country could not retain the morality necessary for a democratic form of government. According to Horace Mann (1796–1859), a prominent education reformer from Massachusetts who advocated the opening of the school day with Bible readings and devotional exercises, "No community can long subsist, unless it has religious principle as the foundation of moral action." Despite objections by Roman Catholics and a minority of Protestants who believed that proper religious instruction involved doctrinal teaching in addition to Bible reading, the inclusion of the Bible and devotional exercises in public schools became established practice throughout the United States. One of the principal reasons was the reverence of the nation's citizens for the Bible.

In addition to the Bible's ethical teaching and its importance for social stability, another reason for the book's exalted status was the way its usage dovetailed with American norms of popular sovereignty. When President Cleveland commented that the Bible was good enough for him, he added that he did not want "notes or criticism, or explanations about authorship or origin or even cross-references." The Bible did not need such help, he added, and more often than not such commentary was confusing. Although Cleveland's logic is not without its own confusion, his outlook was widespread. It developed in the early nineteenth century after American independence and reflected the application of American political ideals to religious life. The simple point behind reading the Bible without assistance from clergy or scholars was the one taught in part by the Revolution: if people were capable of governing themselves, they could also read the Bible for themselves; and if the people did not need a king to rule them and provide stability, they also did not need clergy or priests to tell them how to read the Bible.

This distrust of mediated authority, whether political or religious, had a number of consequences for American attitudes toward the Bible. One of the most important was to attribute the Bible's uniqueness and superiority to its divine nature. In other words, the Bible was authoritative not because it was the words of men, however smart they may have been, but because it was the word of God. The book's divine status thereby allowed Bible believers to avoid the problem raised by the American Revolution, namely, whether and in what form human authority is legitimate. Because of the Bible's divine origins, readers could have direct access to moral and religious truth without assistance from such human authorities as pastors, priests, teachers, or even Bible experts. Consequently Americans came to regard the Bible as a unique book because of its divine origin. All other books of wisdom or morality were flawed because they were written by mere men and women.

The Bible's divinity came in for serious reconsideration during the late nineteenth century. From 1870 until 1900 American colleges and universities, which had been oriented toward the professions of law, medicine, and pastoral ministry, expanded the curriculum dramatically in an effort to accommodate the latest discoveries in the natural and social sciences and to train leaders for America's modernizing society. Similarly the Protestant churches that had been responsible for most of the higher education in the United States adjusted their teachings to the new learning. Chief among these adjustments was a recognition of the Bible's human origins, its similarity to the sacred books of other religions, and its conflict with science. The discoveries of Charles Darwin were one factor in the move by Protestants, even devout ones, to read the Bible less literally and more in harmony with recent discoveries about human origins. During the late nineteenth century, Protestants chose much more frequently than they had in previous centuries to read the Bible as the thoughts and feelings of a religiously inspired people, both ancient Jews and early Christians, who were completely unfamiliar with scientific ways of understanding the world. As such, the Bible became a collection of religious sayings by pious people from antiquity, but it could no longer be considered the literal Word of God. Because of questions raised about the Bible's divine origins, the book lost its uniqueness. The Bible was still worth revering because of its moral and spiritual truths, but discoveries about the book's human authors, combined with the rising authority of the natural sciences, undetermined its teachings on other secular subjects.

The new learning about the Bible also had important implications for a related, though somewhat tangential, evangelical conviction—the nature of conversion. Scholars and ministers who accommodated the new ideas about the Bible still maintained that the Scriptures provided the correct guidelines for ethical and spiritual life. Being good depended in part on believing and following the Bible. Yet, in contrast to the evangelical conviction that goodness was the result of God's activity upon the soul through conversion, the new attitude toward the Bible implied that men and women could follow its teachings apart from divine intervention in the form of a dramatic conversion. In fact, the lives of Christians paralleled the origins of the Bible. If the book could still be the best

source of spiritual and moral counsel, even though it originated from the somewhat backward views of ancient Israelites
and Christians, modern-day believers could also embody god-
liness without divine intervention. This new way of regarding
the Bible gave greater plausibility to the ideas of Horace Bushnell (1802–1876), a Congregationalist minister in Hartford. In
the decades after his death, his ideas influenced a generation
of theologians and biblical scholars in the Northeast who tried
to harmonize Christianity and the new learning. As early as
1847 Bushnell had questioned the revivalist idea of conversion, substituting for it the notion of Christian nurture as a
means of cultivating faith in children from an early age. Over
time his understanding of nurture had greater appeal to
Protestants for whom the conversion experience was impossible. Bushnell's idea of nurture also opened the way for some
Protestant thinkers to abandon Christian teaching about the
sinfulness of human nature. If conversion was unnecessary,
and if children could be encouraged to grow up as Christians,
it followed that human beings were born with an inherent
goodness that faith would help cultivate and improve.

These challenges to the divine character of evangelical
Protestantism, both to its authoritative book and to its decisive
rite of initiation, were precisely the factors that contributed to
the so-called fundamentalist controversy in the Protestant
churches. That it took so long for views that had been familiar
since the 1880s to foment a prolonged and much publicized
conflict is testimony to the relative isolation of the new learning from most Protestants and to the generally activist orientation of the churches during the Progressive Era. Many
evangelicals were so busy in their churches and communities
that they did not notice what the new learning was doing to
the seminaries where their ministers trained. But America's
involvement in World War I changed all that. In the after-

math of the conflict, as evangelicals fretted over the well-being of their churches and nation, they responded with a vigorous assertion of the Bible's and their own faith's divine origins.

During the Great War, Germany was the Allies' enemy. It also served evangelical Protestants as the symbol of the new views about the Bible. German biblical scholarship had been at the forefront of doctrinal innovation and an object of suspicion among some conservatives. But once German armies threatened Western civilization, evangelicals detected a link between bad theology and cultural barbarity. This connection promoted fears about the effects of the new theology on American society, fears that were well on display in 1919 at the first meeting of the World Christian Fundamentals Association. According to William Bell Riley (1861–1947), a prominent Baptist minister in Minneapolis and organizer of the association, liberal Protestants were guilty of infidelity for asserting that the Bible, instead of being inspired by God, "came up out of the human heart." In response to this obvious error, the leaders of the WCFA developed a nine-point platform, of which the chief article was the following: "We believe in the Scripture of the Old and New Testaments as verbally inspired of God, and inerrant in the original writings, and that they are of supreme and final authority in faith and life." The logic for evangelicals was simple. As a human product the Bible was unreliable, but if it were from God it was without error, completely dependable, and the rule for all of life.

In its simplest forms, the emphasis upon the divine nature of the Bible could involve predictable assertions that Christians had affirmed since the ancient church. For instance, the second article of belief in the WCFA's platform was an affirmation of the doctrine of the Trinity: "We believe in one God, eternally existing in three persons, Father, Son, and Holy Spirit." Following this were several points about the person and work of Jesus Christ, such as his being born of a virgin, his death as a sacrifice for sins, and his resurrection from the dead. These were not bizarre beliefs but were in fact the teachings of Protestants and Catholics throughout Christian history. In this sense, evangelicals were in the mainstream of historic Christian teaching.

But this was only part of the story. The leaders of the emerging evangelical outlook also affirmed a number of teachings and practices that were novel and that quickly set conservative Protestants apart from their liberal or modernist foes. One of these beliefs, contained in the WCFA's doctrinal platform, was referred to as "the blessed hope," or what is now known as dispensationalism.* This stood for a peculiar understanding of Christ's second coming that emphasized the moral decline of civilized nations and a cataclysmic end to human history, with Christian believers being raptured (literally ascending into the sky) to greet the return of their Savior. Another conviction that soon occupied the WCFA's leaders was an eccentric understanding of creation that stressed the instantaneous and miraculous activity of God in the formation of Adam and Eve's bodies. In both cases the kind of divine intervention that evangelicals believed was necessary for conversion and revivals also became the only way to explain the beginning and end of time. So even as they were in the mainstream on some Christian teachings, evangelicals were moving to the margins of American Protestantism. Their understanding of creation and the second coming of Christ

*Dispensationalism is the term that proponents of this system applied to their specific brand of biblical interpretation. John Nelson Darby (1800–1882), a priest in the Church of England who left to join the Plymouth Brethren, was the first person to stress seven distinct dispensations (or eras) in biblical history. Over the course of the nineteenth century, this emphasis became known by its proponents and critics as dispensationalism.

emphasized the extraordinary and direct activity of God, as opposed to the processes of nature and human history. As if to compensate for the attention that biblical scholars and scientists were giving to the ordinary character of the Bible, evangelicals stressed the miraculous aspects of Christianity.

One of the speakers at the first meeting of the WCFA was Lewis Sperry Chafer (1871–1952), identified in the program as a "rarely gifted Bible teacher." When he was not speaking at conferences, Chafer pursued an extensive program of instruction in the system of doctrine known as dispensationalism. In fact, he was one of the prominent popularizers and institution-builders of the method of biblical interpretation that would dominate twentieth-century evangelicalism. A native of Ohio and a Congregationalist minister, Chafer's religious roots were firmly planted in the kind of devotion that Dwight L. Moody, revivalist extraordinary, had popularized during the last decades of the nineteenth century. Chafer was committed to winning new converts and improving believers' understanding of the Bible. About the time of the first WCFA meeting, he moved from Buffalo to New York City and became a full-time Bible teacher, offering courses primarily by extension. In 1922 he moved to Dallas, Texas, and two years later founded the Dallas Theological Seminary, the intellectual headquarters for dispensationalism.

At the heart of Chafer's system of instruction was a way of putting the different pieces of the Bible together. According to Christianity, the Bible reveals one religion, but the trick was how to make the Judaism of the Old Testament and the Christianity of the New Testament a unified whole. Chafer's teaching emphasized the differences between the Old and New Testaments and offered a method of charting the Christian church's fortunes in the contemporary era. The church would not possess a national kingdom the way Israel did in the Old Testament; instead Christianity would be apolitical, and its adherents would be socially marginal and sometimes persecuted by earthly powers. This was the church's fate between the first appearance of Christ and his second coming at the end of history. But when Christ returned, according to Chafer, Christians would then be part of a kingdom with infinitely more power and glory than anything Israel in the Old Testament had ever experienced. Because of the hope and expectations surrounding Christ's second coming, dispensationalism became famous for its interpretation of biblical passages (that is, prophecy) that predicted when and how the end of human history would occur.

Chafer's system of doctrine was virtually unknown in mainstream theological circles but immensely popular among the Protestant laity. Dispensationalism's appeal was ironic since some of its teachings were no less complex than those propounded in the halls of university divinity schools and seminaries. Yet it thrived in settings where a college degree was not required for admission—in large-scale meetings and Bible conferences where average men and women could spend a few hours in song and Bible study and be encouraged that, no matter how bad things might be, Christ was in control of history and orchestrating the world's affairs for the ultimate good of believers. What was particularly appealing about dispensationalism was that for all its complexity, it seemed to return the Bible to the people and its meaning to the book's plain sense. Since the sixteenth century, Protestants had affirmed that the Bible's meaning was clear and accessible even to the most ordinary of intellects. The new scholarship on the humanness of the Bible seemed to come between the people and God's word, as if, as one evangelical pastor put it, common folks had to "await a communication from Tübingen or a telegram from Oxford before [they could] read the Bible." Consequently, even if the speculations of dispensationalism's proponents about world affairs could sound bizarre, this system of biblical interpretation kept alive the American Protestant tradition of populist Christianity where all readings of the Bible were equal, with preference for the one most popular.

Dispensationalism also appealed to Protestants who had legitimate fears about the direction of American society. The last decades of the nineteenth century and the first ones of the twentieth were marked by great advances in physical comfort thanks to the economic growth and technological improvements associated with urbanization and industrialization. These changes in American society also yielded genuine suffering. Whether because of the difficult living conditions faced by immigrants or the social and economic dislocation experienced by native-stock Americans, the modernization of American society raised a myriad of questions about whether the nation was in fact improving or careening out of control. America's entrance into World War I only reinforced this sense of crisis and extended these questions beyond national to international relations. But what made the war particularly significant for evangelicals was its apparent confirmation of dispensationalist interpretation. For years at Bible prophecy conferences across the United States, speakers had used portions of the Old and New Testaments to make predictions about how the end of history would occur. These scenarios always involved conflicts in Europe and the Middle East. With the Great War in Europe came proof positive not only that the Bible was right but that the return of Christ was near. In effect, World War I put an exclamation point on the social and political turmoil that was making dispensationalism plausible and appealing to evangelical Protestants.

Of course, not every Protestant believed the dispensationalist scenario of human history and its imminent finale. Indeed, every aspect of change that evangelicals regarded as a indication of decline, other Protestants, many of whom were modernists, saw as progress. The very name "modernist

Protestant" suggested an outlook favorable to the kinds of developments that were transforming American society. Modernist leaders believed that the teachings of Christianity needed to be adapted and upgraded for modern consumption. The churches needed to be in the vanguard of social change, not merely reactive and defensive to all things new. What is more, modernists held that human history was gradually improving, not simply because living conditions were advancing but also because God was active and present in the forces of social, political, economic, and cultural life. This outlook was sometimes called postmillennialism, and it stood in marked contrast to evangelical beliefs about Christ's return.

For many modernists, the millennium, the time of Christ's thousand-year reign and a period of peace and righteousness, was gradually unfolding as human history progressed. The kingdom of God was especially evident in Western civilization, where advances in medicine, science, politics, and technology were preparing a more equitable, peaceful, and moral society. The return of Christ, accordingly, would take place at the end of a prolonged period of peace and righteousness. One did not have to be a liberal Protestant to believe in such a scheme for historical development. Mainstream Protestants throughout the nineteenth century thought that human history was progressing in such a beneficial way and that America itself was ushering in the kingdom of God. But during the late nineteenth and early twentieth centuries, this perception took on added momentum thanks to the teaching of religious modernists. In this view, not only missions, revivals, and Bible reading but also such human endeavors as education, philanthropy, the arts, science, and medicine contributed to the religious aim of Christ's reign because God was present in the unfolding of all aspects of human history—at least in benevolent ones.

Dispensationalism taught evangelicals to break with such

progressive notions. It offered a bracing jolt of pessimism. As evangelical leaders rightly noted, many of the advances in human arts and sciences, along with larger social developments, were scarcely free from negative side effects. World War I was evidence that the alleged advances of Western civilization could result in horrible forms of destruction and that the most civilized nations on earth were capable of remarkable brutality. So for every sign of progress, dispensationalism invariably saw at least two steps backward. Thus the return of Christ could not be expected at the end of a sustained period of prosperity and righteousness. Human beings were incapable of making such advances. Instead God would have to intervene mightily to make things right. The millennium, according to dispensationalist teaching, would come not before but after Christ's return. In the meantime, as the prophecies of the Bible foretold from both the Old and New Testaments, the conditions of human society would only worsen. In fact, one of the many ways Christians could know that the end of history and Christ's return was near was by the degree to which society deteriorated. In the last days, as dispensationalist teachers like Chafer reminded audience, wars, famines, pestilence, immorality, and tyranny would be obvious and widespread. These dire circumstances would emphasize the wickedness of human endeavor and the need for God's activity to make things right. This was a forceful rationale for evangelism and revivals. Because the times were so unsettling, evangelicals could point to contemporary crises as part of the reason for nonbelievers to convert and for evangelicals themselves to be more vigilant in spreading the message of Christianity.

Dispensationalism also reinforced the dichotomy that evangelicalism marked off between the human and the divine. Not only did evangelicals reject the idea that the Bible was the product of human authors—as opposed to God's word—thanks to dispensationalism they looked to God's supernatural intervention into human affairs as the only hope to remedy evil. In other words, human endeavor became all the more suspect, not simply because of the defective teaching of wayward preachers but because history was proving yet again that men and women were sinful, their efforts to improve society were utopian, and any lasting solution to human suffering or immorality was impossible without God's immediate and drastic work of grace.

Evangelicals' pessimistic view of historical development quickened into the 1930s and became even more pronounced in the 1940s, thanks to the evidence provided by the Great Depression and another world war. Radio became an important outlet for educating the laity with news about the end of history and Christ's imminent return. Three of the era's most popular radio evangelists, Harry Ironside of Chicago's Moody Memorial Church, Donald Grey Barnhouse of Philadelphia's Tenth Presbyterian Church, and Charles Fuller's *Old Fashioned Revival Hour*, broadcast from California, had all accepted dispensationalist teaching and spread the word to national audiences. An excerpt from *History's Crowded Climax*, a book written during the 1930s by Arthur Maxwell, editor of *Signs of the Times*, suggests why the message of dispensationalism was so attractive:

> With wars raging all about us, with civilization threatened with complete destruction, with all the world plunged once more into the utmost confusion, it is a great consolation to reflect that there are some things which will definitely outlast all earthly conflicts.... However dark and forbidding the world situation may appear—and it is surely dark enough today—God still rules in heaven ..., quietly and patiently working out His eternal purpose.

For Americans who were not as affluent as some in the main-line churches, the message of evangelical preachers and writers—that no matter how bad conditions became, God was still in control and the return of Christ would make things right—was indeed welcome news.

The triumph of evolution in American education reinforced the sense of cultural crisis that dispensationalism nurtured among evangelicals. Darwinian notions of human origins provided tangible evidence of what was wrong with American society. At the same time a concerted campaign against teaching evolution in the public schools gave evangelicals a platform upon which to voice their sense of alienation. (Ironically, the sort of cultural pessimism that dispensationalism bequeathed to evangelicals also rendered pointless their efforts to remove the teaching of evolution from public school curricula. If Christ's return were imminent, what difference would better public schools make in the cosmic contest between good and evil?) The tension between dispensationalism and evolution was particularly evident in the life of the WCFA. After its founding in 1919, the leaders of the association hoped to make it an umbrella organization for all conservative Protestants, in opposition to the existing ecumenical Protestant agencies which evangelicals believed were infiltrated by modernists. But by 1923, when such hopes looked unrealistic, leaders of the WCFA turned from driving liberal theology out of the churches to forcing evolution from the public schools.

The shift to evolution was no publicity stunt, however, since the progress that biologists charted in nature had been appropriated by ministers and theologians to support the idea that the kingdom of God was progressing within Western civilization. Since the late nineteenth century, a generation of college-educated Americans had learned that the general direction of every part of creation, from nature to society, was one of gradual progress. Just as human beings had evolved from lower forms of life, so democracy had emerged from oppressive forms of government, religion from unenlightened patterns of belief—the list was endless. By questioning this progressive and optimistic scheme with dispensationalism's prediction of warfare, pestilence, and suffering, evangelicals raised an important objection to evolutionary logic. And if progress were not inevitable in society, the improvement of nature according to some vague organic plan, no matter what biologists were saying, was no more certain.

Evangelical objections to evolution went beyond an intuitive pessimism about the possibility of progress. Another piece of the argument against biological accounts of human origins was the conviction, already noted in connection with evangelical beliefs about the Bible, that divine activity was ordinarily supernatural or miraculous. Just as evangelicals preserved the Bible's uniqueness by stressing the book's divine qualities, when it came to the creation of the world they likewise objected to efforts that explained human origins as part of a natural process. For evangelicals, God's actions could never be reduced to such ordinary proportions. As one evangelical minister put it, evolution "denies the supernatural in the scheme and process of life. It finds no place for a miracle, or a miracle-working God." This minister went on to deduce that if the first Adam possessed such natural origins, the same applied to the second Adam, Jesus Christ. And for that reason he concluded that evolution was not simply a threat to the Bible's teaching about creation; it "of necessity" denied "the deity of Christ." Evangelicals were intent on preserving the supernatural and therefore the divine character of their religion. Positing a naturalistic account of one part of the Bible's teaching—in this case, creation—inevitably undermined the most revered articles of faith, such as the deity of Christ. If the Bible, Christ, and the creation of man and woman were not supernatural in their origins, according to evangelical logic they were not divine and therefore uncertain if not false.

The stress upon the divine also had implications for the evangelical conception of human nature, the other notable component in the rejection of evolution. The notion that human beings had descended from apes, evangelical leaders were quick to point out, destroyed whatever tattered threads of civilization remained and would inevitably turn respectable men and women into barbarians, just as Darwinism had ruined Germany during World War I. As one evangelical leader put it, evolution robbed "man of his spiritual nature and makes him a developed beast." In other words, biology removed all consideration of humankind's spiritual nature, the one link it possessed to the divine and to the possibility of morality. Evangelical fears about evolution's implications for decency and morality help explain the repeated references to students, whether college or high school, and what a steady diet of Darwin's thought would do to future generations. If social science surveys demonstrated a decline of belief in God among college students, could any plausible explanation exist other than the teaching of evolution? Surely, according to William Jennings Bryan, the evidence of spiritual decline at America's colleges and universities was compelling. But even worse than the effects of evolution upon individuals was what had happened collectively to societies under the new science's influence. The reason for World War I, Bryan argued, was not ignorance but science of the wrong kind. "Scientists mixed the poisonous gases and manufactured liquid fire. Intellect guided the nations, and learning without heart made war so hellish that civilization itself was about to commit suicide." Evolution contained the seeds of science's immorality, but the preservation of biblical teaching would restore order and ethical norms to American society as well as to the fraternity of nations.

Although evangelicals' views on creation appeared to suffer defeat in the public realm thanks to the way Bryan's critics in court and in the press ridiculed him at the Scopes Trial, anti-evolutionism would not go away. In fact it grew more popular into the next decade. The two men most responsible for creationism's appeal were the would-be scientists Harry Rimmer (1890–1952), a Presbyterian minister and extraordinary debater, and George McCready Price (1870–1963), a Seventh-Day Adventist professor of geology and philosophy. Both men had an ability to turn the defense of Genesis and biblical morality into an apparently scientific argument. In Rimmer's and Price's hands, the belief in the biblical account of creation became "scientific creationism." Rimmer accomplished this primarily by pointing out the inconsistencies of science, often pitting the findings of biologists against physicists or geologists. He was also a gifted speaker whose skills in debate could make up for his scientific ignorance and give him the advantage in highly publicized contests with prominent scientists. The effect of Rimmer's argument was to raise a sufficient number of questions about the "assured" results of scientific investigation and then to reassure the faithful that the Bible was the surest guide on matters of creation. Price's influence came largely through his writings, notably his use of the Genesis account of the flood to raise questions about the geological record. If the layers of fossils that geologists had discovered did not follow a sequential pattern because of a universal flood that had overturned and reordered the whole earth's surface, Price reasoned that the biblical account of creation may have been much more reliable than scientists supposed. By drawing on scientific data, Price and Rimmer gave evangelicals the sense that their faith did indeed harmonize with modern science, and that the unbelief of the mainstream scientific community was more a function of anti-religious prejudice than of superior knowledge.

One sign of the effort to make evangelicalism scientifically respectable after the Scopes Trial was the formation in 1935 of the Religion and Science Association (RSA). This organization, in which Price played a prominent role, was formed to bring unity to evangelicals and to provide an alternative professional scientific body for God-fearing Christians. Although the hoped-for cooperation among scientifically interested evangelicals never materialized, the RSA was a harbinger of future evangelical intellectual developments. In response to the dominance of secular or nonbiblical points of view in the world of American learning, evangelicals founded alternative learned societies that provided space for believing scholars to maintain their religious convictions while studying God's creation. A year after the RSA fell apart in 1937, evangelical scientists formed the Deluge Geology Society and espoused the narrower view that God had created the earth in six literal days. Over time a more mainstream evangelical scientific organization, the American Scientific Affiliation, founded in 1951, provided still another outlet for believing scientists. Natural science was not the only interest of evangelicals. In 1949 they also established the Evangelical Theological Society, a group dedicated to biblical scholarship that emphasized the Bible as God's word, free from errors, scientific or historical. Whatever the long-term effect of these bodies, their immediate impact was to reinforce the perception that evangelicals were, if not odd, at least different from the rest of American society, and that the reason for this difference was their belief in and interpretation of the Bible.

As odd as evangelicals may have appeared on the eve of World War II, these Protestants were virtually indistinguishable from the believers who in the nineteenth century had formed the dominant religious faith in the United States. As early as 1844 Robert Baird, one of the first historians of Christianity in

America, described the convictions that united the majority of Protestants. These included the doctrines of the Trinity and atonement, a similar understanding of the morality by which believers should live, and the necessity of undergoing a conversion experience or what he called being "born again." Almost fifty years later another church historian described American Protestantism in similar terms. According to H. K. Carroll, writing in 1893, the beliefs that united all Protestants under the umbrella of evangelicalism were the "inspiration, authority and sufficiency" of the Bible, the Trinity, the deity of Christ, justification "by faith alone," and the work of the Holy Spirit "in the conversion and sanctification of the sinner." Twentieth-century evangelicals such as Riley, Chafer, Bryan, Rimmer, and Price would have had no trouble agreeing with any part of these doctrinal platforms. Yet by the 1930s the religion that had once been sufficiently broad to unite Protestants in a variety of political, social, and religious undertakings had become the faith of the Protestant fringe.

Evidence of the fractured state of American Protestantism was readily available in church life during the 1920s. The most publicized skirmishes occurred in the northern Baptist and Presbyterian denominations, where some of the major public advocates of the fundamentalist cause were also active. For instance, Riley was an important spokesman for fundamentalists in the Northern Baptist Convention. These conservative Baptists feared a weakening of theological rigor in Baptist seminaries and a watering down of the church's message among foreign missionaries. Likewise, Bryan spoke for many conservative Presbyterians in the northern Presbyterian church (Presbyterian Church in the U.S.A.) who also took issue with liberal theology in Presbyterian seminaries and with theological relativism on the mission field.

Spotting the line where worries about evolution in public schools or immorality in American society ended and internal denominational matters began was—and still is—a difficult task. But the debates among Baptists and Presbyterians in the North gained more attention from the media precisely because the lines separating the Protestant churches and American society were neither straight nor clear. Even so, Methodists, Episcopalians, Reformed, and Lutherans, along with Southern Baptists, experienced conflicts during the 1920s that scholars typically add together to comprise the fundamentalist controversy. The net effect of these debates, several of which launched new denominations (for example, the General Association of Regular Baptists [1932], the Orthodox Presbyterian Church [1936], and the Conservative Baptist Convention [1947]), was to polarize what had been the solid religious block of mainstream American Protestantism. Where members of the largest denominations had once recognized other Protestants as partners in a common project of protecting Christian civilization in America and promoting the true faith around the world through foreign missionaries, after the 1920s American Protestants became openly suspicious and critical of fellow members. Conservatives complained of liberal errors, and liberals of conservative sectarianism.

An important factor in this development was the way twentieth-century evangelicals responded to the intellectual threats that the new learning posed for the Bible. The problem was not simply that scholars had cultivated an outlook among the college-educated that made belief in the Bible implausible. Evangelicals also compounded the difficulty by defending the Bible in ways that left little room for negotiation. For them the Bible was a divine book. It was not only free from error but showed little if any trace of human influence. At the same time the Bible revealed truths that completely overturned the findings of science. The Bible's explanation of the creation of man and woman rested upon the work of instantaneous divine intervention, which was necessary if Western civilization were to be preserved. Furthermore the Bible, according to evangelical interpretation, contradicted any notion of social progress based upon human agency. In fact, thanks to human sinfulness, the general tendency of history, according to evangelicals, was toward decline. As a result, beliefs about and interpretation of the Bible contributed greatly to the marginalization of evangelicalism during the first half of the twentieth century.

As offbeat as their understanding of the Bible was, the book's divine character and its teaching about creation and Christ's second coming gave evangelicals a sense of identity, intellectual unity, and common purpose. It transformed a group of Protestants from a rather diverse set of backgrounds into a seemingly identifiable mass movement. One of the clearest indications of the emergence of evangelicalism as a distinctive subset of American Protestantism was the infrastructure of educational institutions that functioned as the intellectual guardians of the movement. Leading the way were Bible colleges, followed by seminaries and then liberal arts colleges some distance from the front. What made these evangelical institutions unique was again their understanding of the Bible.

Before the twentieth century evangelicals had been at the forefront of American higher education. Before 1870, in fact, the leading institutions of higher learning were practically all Protestant in origin. Their mission had been to train the leaders of American society with specific attention to the professions of medicine, law, and divinity. Religion was part and parcel of the nineteenth-century college, with required attendance at chapel and Sunday worship. Most faculty and administrators were clergy; and a senior-year course in moral philosophy, taught by the president, tied the entire curriculum together from a Christian perspective. But during the last three decades of the nineteenth century the mantle of leadership in American higher education passed from denominational colleges to research universities. Part of the reason for this change was an effort by educators to adapt higher education to the new realities of an urbanizing and industrializing America. The nation needed more than lawyers, physicians, and clergy if it was to become an important player in world politics; it also needed, for instance, engineers, social scientists, managers, chemists—the list could go on—for the country to develop as a fully modern society. University leaders responded to this need by expanding the curriculum of higher education beyond the humanities and languages to embrace the natural and social sciences, and by providing graduate training in specialized academic disciplines. The effect of these profound changes—some have called it a secular revolution—was to make religion marginal to the mission of colleges and universities. The spiritual tenor of these schools changed. Believers in the late nineteenth century who sought institutions that would defend the truth of the Bible and prepare Christian workers to carry out the mission of the church, as evangelicals most certainly did, were forced to look to schools other than the mainstream colleges and first-rate universities.

One of the first signs of an alternative to the "secular" institutions was the formation of Bible institutes and colleges in the last decades of the nineteenth century. The earliest examples were the Missionary Training Institute, founded in 1882 by A. B. Simpson and located in New York City, and the Moody Bible Institute, which began four years later in Chicago under the auspices of the famous urban evangelist Dwight L. Moody. Within the next four decades similar institutions emerged, with those in Los Angeles, Detroit, Minneapolis, Boston, and Philadelphia the most noteworthy. The urban location of these schools was significant. Bible colleges were designed to train lay workers to be missionaries, evangelists, and religious advocates among the poor and destitute in America's largest cities. An urban location not only made these schools more accessible to greater numbers of evangelicals, it also provided a laboratory for students and faculty to evangelize the large number of city dwellers, recently arrived from Europe and Asia, who appeared to have little acquaintance with the truths of the Bible.

In order to train lay religious workers, Bible institutes emphasized a practical and efficient curriculum which equipped students with the skills they would need in missions and evangelism. Yet as much as these institutions functioned as vocational schools for the laity, the actual content of courses made mastery of the Bible a necessity. In fact, the Bible was the principal textbook. Teachers steeped students in what one writer called "a Bird's-Eye View of the Bible," which meant a holistic overview of the Bible's contents presented according to the dispensationalist scheme of interpretation. Graduates from these schools went away with an encyclopedic knowledge of the Bible's contents, having memorized large sections of the text, able to reproduce outlines of individual books, and ready to speak on any subject with a word from Scripture, especially in the context of evangelism.

Between 1880 and 1920 Bible institutes more or less coexisted with the diversity of colleges and universities, whether religious or secular, available to evangelicals. But by the 1920s, when the debates over creation apparently revealed the godless direction of American higher education, even among Protestant denominational colleges, Bible institutes became the evangelical alternative for education beyond high school. Between 1918 and 1945 evangelicals founded seventy new Bible schools. This self-imposed intellectual exile was important for two reasons. First, it emphasized the division that evangelicals explicitly drew between the study of the Bible and other areas of human inquiry. Bible colleges divorced the study of the Bible, a religious enterprise, from the study of nature, human nature, and society, the so-called secular disciplines. Whether intended or not, such a divorce ironically reinforced the very process of secularization that evangelicals opposed.

Second, the increasing popularity of Bible colleges among evangelicals signaled a marked indifference to anything other than the Bible and vocations other than evangelism. This is not to say that individual evangelicals were uninterested in politics, sports, the stock market, or fashion. Still, the message communicated by Bible colleges and their graduates was a dualistic one: the world and its affairs were in fundamental tension with the Bible and its demands for soul-winning and holy living. In sum, the intellectual universe of evangelicals, a fairly wide terrain during the nineteenth century, shrank considerably during the first half of the twentieth century. It included little more than Bible study and the most effective means of evangelizing.

Bible colleges and institutes were not the only places where evangelicals could hone their understanding of the Bible. Seminaries such as Chafer's Dallas Theological Seminary and Westminster in Philadelphia, founded in 1929, provided education for college-educated men intent on being pastors, an occupation that had elitist connotations to the evangelical rank and file who were generally more comfortable with lay workers. Since all believers, according to evangelical notions of work, were supposed to know their Bible well and also be able to communicate Christian truths to others, the idea of a separate order of professionals trained to dispense biblical wisdom appeared to be a waste of precious resources. Only after World War II, when parts of the evangelical constituency began to participate in the larger expansion of American higher education and the socioeconomic opportunities that accompanied it, did evangelical seminaries begin to grow and gain the honor previously reserved for Bible colleges.

Even so, during the first half of the twentieth century, theological education at places such as Dallas and Westminster reinforced evangelical zeal for the Bible as the fountain of all truth and hope. As already observed, under Chafer's leadership Dallas emerged as the intellectual center of dispensationalism. At first the school sought to train pastors primarily for the southern Presbyterian Church (PCUS). But after an investigation by the denomination severed informal ties to the seminary, Dallas's faculty and students came from and returned to the nondenominational network of churches and schools that had grown up around the Bible prophecy conference movement of the late nineteenth century. In contrast, Westminster Seminary had strong ties to the Orthodox Presbyterian Church, a denomination that left the northern Presbyterian Church (PCUSA) in 1936 in the wake of the fundamentalist controversy. Although Westminster rejected most of dispensationalism's tenets in favor of historic Presbyterianism, the school made its mark in the wider world of conservative Protestantism through its defense of the truth and infallibility of the Bible. Conservative Presbyterian arguments on behalf of the Bible's divinity could be difficult reading, as such collections of essays by Westminster faculty as *The Infallible Word* (1946) attested. The interaction in this book with serious theological scholarship, both old and modern, was impressive. Still, for all its thoughtfulness, such learning did little to help evangelicals see the importance of matters other than the Bible.

Because of the heavy emphasis on the Bible as the lone voice of stability and truth, few evangelical liberal arts colleges existed. Where they did, they often felt more like Bible colleges that offered enough supplemental course work to qualify for a bachelor of arts degree. Again, part of the reason for the mediocrity of evangelical colleges during the first half of the twentieth century was that they competed in a tough market. Most denominations had their own colleges, and before World War II the number of Americans going on for study beyond high school was never higher than 5 percent. Even so, the cultural pessimism that dispensationalism nurtured, when combined with a suspicion of truths not confirmed by the Bible, left evangelicals with a mental universe that made it difficult to appreciate the physics of an Albert Einstein, the literary theories or poetry of a T. S. Eliot, or the anthropological insights of a Franz Boas. As late as the 1950s, biologists at Wheaton College in Illinois could draw the ire of trustees for endeavoring to interpret Genesis in a way more compatible with evolution, thus demonstrating the handicaps under which evangelical liberal arts colleges operated thanks to the movement's special interpretation of the Bible.

By the 1940s some evangelicals showed signs of restlessness with their inherited intellectual straitjacket. One such evangelical was Carl F. H. Henry (1913–), who at the time was fresh out of graduate school with a Ph.D. in philosophy but who would emerge in the second half of the twentieth century as one of evangelicalism's most articulate theological spokesmen. His important little book, *The Uneasy Conscience of Modern Fundamentalism* (1947), was the first notable call for evangelicals to enlarge their intellectual horizons beyond the Bible and the specific theories derived from it about the beginning and end of human history. Henry urged evangelicals to "develop a competent literature in every field of study, on every level from the grade school through the university." This investment, however, would have to wait several decades before paying dividends. Meanwhile evangelicals remained cut off from the wider currents of American culture, thanks to their undying commitment to the Bible. Having witnessed the upheaval generated as much by American prosperity during the late nineteenth century as by world war in the second decade of the twentieth century, evangelicals abandoned the broader expanse of modern learning to hunker down with the solid and lasting truths taught by a divinely inspired book. Such isolation was a far cry from the approbation that evangelicalism had enjoyed in the United States before the Civil War. But it may have been the only possible outcome of a system of religious reflection uncertain about its direction without direct guidance from holy writ.

2

The Formation of an Evangelical Subculture

DEVOUT CHRISTIANS AND JEWS have long opposed the practice of mixed marriage. In order to maintain the integrity of the believing community, pastors, priests, and rabbis have instructed the faithful to avoid romantic relationships with individuals outside the faith. For Christians, one of the reliable places to substantiate the importance of believers marrying only among themselves is the second letter of the apostle Paul to the church at Corinth. In 2 Corinthians 6:17 he writes, ". . . therefore come out from them, and be separate from them, says the Lord." Interestingly enough, Paul is quoting here from the Jewish scriptures the words of the prophet Isaiah (52:11), thus linking Christian prohibitions against mixed marriages to the practice of the Israelites.

For twentieth-century evangelicals, marriage was just a small part of what the prophet Isaiah and the apostle Paul had in mind when it came to avoiding unwholesome alliances. Paul's admonition in the letter to the church at Corinth became a common refrain in the writings of evangelical leaders during the years between 1925 and 1960. Not only were evangelical adolescents and single young adults warned about the danger of marrying a nonbeliever; evangelicals in all walks of life received repeated instruction about the harmful influence of the world and its culture on efforts to lead a holy life. Evangelicals were to lead lives free from unholy alliances with the world.

The most notable instance of evangelical separatism came in the early 1940s when conservative Protestants looked to pick up the pieces of their failed crusades of the 1920s and 1930s to reform America's largest Protestant denominations. The biggest battles had occurred in the northern Baptist and Presbyterian denominations, and in both cases fundamentalists had suffered decisive defeats that also led to the formation of new conservative denominations. For other evangelicals, withdrawal from mainstream Protestantism happened in a less intentional manner—here and there a congregation would simply sever its ties to the national denominational structures. By 1940 leading conservatives looked for organizations that could unite the various conservative denominations and congregations into a cooperative whole which would challenge the modernist errors of the mainline Protestant churches and restore a vigorous Christian voice in American society.

The question that quickly emerged during these attempts at evangelical cooperation concerned the nature of separation. Some evangelicals, such as Carl McIntire (1906–2002), who in 1941 organized the American Council of Christian Churches, insisted that a truly evangelical church could have nothing to do with the mainline churches. This meant that any denomination or congregation joining with McIntire could not also be a member of the Federal Council of Churches, which was mainstream Protestantism's ecumenical agency. Other evangelicals, such as the ones who in 1942 formed the National Association of Evangelicals, hoped to unite conservatives in all denominations, including those who may have chosen to remain in a liberal denomination. The issue, then, was what sort of separation the Bible required. Was it a form of compromise

to continue to cooperate with mainline Protestants while joining with other conservatives in an evangelical organization?
Or was it possible to be separate from the world even while re-
maining in a mainline denomination, as long as one remained
an evangelical?

Although evangelicals answered these questions differently—more joined the National Association of Evangelicals
than the American Council of Christian Churches—born-
again Protestants had a clear sense that their faith required
separation from the wider culture. The ideas informing this
sense of cultural withdrawal were a mix of biblical interpretation and cultural anxiety. But the practice of separatism was
not mixed. At a time when economic and political developments could very well have stifled initiative, evangelicals
established a number of institutions that were designed to
reinforce the necessity of conversion and evangelism, the importance of Bible study, and the duty of holy living. The
subculture that evangelicals built went unnoticed by many observers of American religion. But it provided the building
blocks for a later attempt to extend evangelical norms beyond
the religious ghetto and reassert an evangelical presence in
American public life.

At the beginning of the 1930s the idea of evangelicalism as a
spent force in American life was one that occurred naturally
to those who had witnessed the religious controversies of the
1920s. Not only had evangelicals suffered the loss of a prominent spokesman, William Jennings Bryan, who died only days
after the embarrassment of the Scopes Trial, but they had also
been repeatedly unsuccessful in various denominational struggles. By the time H. Richard Niebuhr composed an article on
born-again Protestantism for the *Encyclopedia of the Social Sciences* (1937), he could with a measure of confidence write of
evangelicalism in the past tense. The religious conflicts of the

1920s, according to Niebuhr, were the last gasp of rural Protestants in revolt against the progressive march of knowledge, industry, and cities. As American society modernized, evangelicals would continue to wither.

The Protestants about whom Niebuhr wrote may have receded from his view, but they hardly withered during the years between the stock market crash of 1929 and America's entry into World War II. In fact they created a religious subculture whose vitality contradicted the wisdom of America's pundits. Part of the reason for evangelicalism's institutional success can only be explained by the movement's sense of alienation. Having lost two of the most important cultural institutions for a good society, namely, the churches and the schools, many evangelicals looked to create an alternative world that would preserve stability and virtue, if not within the nation, at least among the faithful.

Bible institutes and colleges were pivotal in the construction of a separate evangelical culture. The importance of these institutions extended beyond the way evangelicals thought about the Bible and the world; their wide-ranging activities gave born-again Protestants a sense of identity and purpose. In addition to the certificates and degrees awarded by Bible colleges, they also offered instruction to audiences near and far, first through prophecy conferences and local bookstores, then through magazines and radio stations. Perhaps most surprising to those who associated evangelicals with cultural backwardness was the entrepreneurial side of the movement. Despite the stereotype of being rural and uneducated, Bible college leaders pioneered in the field of religious publishing and broadcasting. For instance, Moody Bible Institute sponsored the magazine *Moody Monthly* and launched the Chicago radio station WMBI. Another example was the Bible Institute of Los Angeles (BIOLA), which published the popular magazine *The King's Business* and started one of the first radio stations in California, KJS. Through measures like these, in some cases old-fashioned and in others breathtakingly new, evangelicals not only displayed an ability to make faith popular, they also established networks through which their convictions could be disseminated. It is not a stretch to think of the constituencies created by the Bible colleges as alternative denominations. In many cases Protestants who had formerly identified with one of the national Protestant church bodies now joined an informal membership of people who read a certain magazine, listened to a specific radio program, and sent financial assistance to a certain Bible institute.

Yet Bible colleges and the ancillary services they offered were not the only means of religious edification available to evangelicals who were disillusioned with the mainline Protestant churches. The Bible conference was another institution that gained in popularity during the 1930s and 1940s, thanks to religious as well as social change. Bible or prophecy conferences, as they were also called, were not entirely separate phenomena from Bible institutes and colleges. The impetus for both conference and institute were the same: making the Bible accessible to the laity according to the teaching of dispensationalist theology. The overlap between the schools and conferences continued in the matter of personnel: the men speaking at the conferences were usually those who taught at the college or institute. Where the Bible conferences differed from these other evangelical endeavors was in their special blend of serious piety and devout recreation. The key word used to describe these conferences was "summer," meaning that attendees could use vacation time to spend a week or two in a resort setting, say in rural New Hampshire or ocean side in Atlantic City, New Jersey, and spend mornings and evenings listening to Bible exposition while using the afternoons to swim, play softball, fish, or hike. The popularity of these vacation spots is hard to determine, but advertisements in *Moody Monthly* show an increase from twenty-seven to just over fifty locations between 1930 and 1941. No doubt part of this expansion stemmed from the increasing affordability of automobiles, which evangelicals used to travel to these centers of religious relaxation.

Another source that reinforced the distinctive ways of evangelicals, again connected to but distinct from the Bible college network, was religious broadcasting. By the 1930s the radio had emerged as one of the more popular forms of entertainment in American society. During the five years after the Great Depression, for instance, the number of radios in homes doubled from roughly nine million to eighteen million. Throughout their history, born-again Protestants had showed a hostility to the constraints of church structures for the work of evangelism and other measures in spreading the gospel. This entrepreneurial streak, which used any and all means for making new converts, found in radio yet another avenue for gaining new adherents. The leadership of the Bible colleges and institutes were among the first to explore religious broadcasting, but soon pastors and evangelists across the United States were producing shows that featured Bible teaching and religious music. Although these programs largely preached to the converted rather than won new converts, their popularity was impossible to deny.

One of the first evangelicals to see the potential of radio and to tap its possibilities was Paul Rader (1878–1938), a college football coach and boxer who upon conversion became a full-time evangelist in Chicago. Rader's notoriety began in 1922 when he founded the Chicago Gospel Tabernacle, a meeting place on the North Side that was not a church and so had no regular membership; but it did hold regular meetings which featured musicians and renowned pastors, almost in the fashion of a religious vaudeville theater. Trips to the "Tab" became a regular part of evangelical life in Chicago since its Sunday

afternoon meetings did not conflict with local worship services. But aside from sanctified showmanship, Rader's real
knack was in the arena of music. He enlisted the services of
Chicago's leading gospel musicians to perform in the Tabernacle band, which accompanied the audience's singing and also
played alone. Rader's feel for music led to the production of
Tabernacle Hymns, a songbook which was adopted by many
evangelical congregations and became a best-seller for Rader's
Tabernacle Publishing Company. Still, the combination of religious exhortation and gospel music did not find its fullest
outlet until 1925 when Rader worked out an arrangement
with Chicago's mayor, William H. Thompson, to broadcast an
all-day Sunday program on Thompson's own radio station,
WHT. Rader's *National Radio Chapel* could be heard as far
away as the East Coast and in parts of Canada. Its success encouraged him to branch out into a number of more specialized
shows, from the *Shepherd Hour*, which featured stories and
songs for youngsters, to the *Request Hour*, on which musicians would play hymns or gospel songs requested by listeners.
The Bible and its message were always in view in Rader's programs. But just as crucial to his success, aside from his own
talent as a speaker, was the mix of entertainment and devotion, especially evident in the predominance of music in these
shows.

Religious music was also a prominent factor in the success
of Charles E. Fuller (1887–1969), whose *Old Fashioned Revival Hour*, based in Los Angeles, reached an audience of fifteen million to twenty million over the Mutual Broadcasting
System. A citrus farmer and dealer, Fuller converted during a
revival led by Paul Rader and thereafter devoted his life to religious work. After studying at the Bible Institute of Los Angeles, he led a home Bible study which eventually grew into
an independent evangelical congregation in Placentia, California, named Calvary Church. Although Fuller had broad-

cast some of his Bible classes on BIOLA's radio station as early as 1924, he began to pursue the medium with seriousness only in 1929, when he first broadcast the evening services of Calvary Church. By 1935 Fuller had left the church to give all his energy to religious broadcasting. His efforts were rewarded in 1937 when the Mutual network contracted with him for a program in prime time on Sunday evenings.

Key to the success of the *Old Fashioned Revival Hour* was Fuller's genius in finding musical talent. He hired the Goose Creek Gospel Quartet and its pianist, Rudy Atwood, to perform gospel hymns in a way far removed from the staid anthems of church choirs. Fuller also had a warm and folksy manner that gave listeners the sense of inviting a trusted friend into their living rooms rather than a loud and threatening evangelist. One of the most compelling features of Fuller's broadcasts was his wife, Grace, who would read excerpts from the audience's letters. She was particularly adept at choosing letters that had a sentimental quality and elicited emotions accompanying death or separation from loved ones. Sometimes Grace would even alter a letter's specifics to give it broader appeal. During World War II the reading of letters from soldiers in Europe and the Pacific increased the domestic and international audience of the "Old Fashioned Revival Hour" through Mutual's expanding network and shortwave radio broadcasts. During the 1940s Fuller's program accounted for one-eighth of the network's revenue and required a budget of close to $2 million. No doubt Fuller's success stemmed from his own skills and marketing savvy. But he also summoned up images of a bygone America, when the folk religion of the nation was easily accessible and down to earth. During a time of economic hardship and international strife, such images were reassuring not simply to evangelicals but to Anglo-Americans generally.

Just as Bible institutes inevitably spun off other religious enterprises, evangelical broadcasting was no different. Here the case of Donald Grey Barnhouse (1895–1960), a pastor of Philadelphia's Tenth Presbyterian Church, is an apt case in point. A California native who headed east for seminary (Princeton Theological Seminary), Barnhouse was a soldier in World War I and remained in Europe for six years after the war as a missionary before returning to the United States as a Presbyterian pastor in Philadelphia. In 1928 he started *The Bible Study Hour*, which though not as popular as Fuller's broadcast nonetheless attracted a national audience. Like many evangelicals, Barnhouse and his staff had entrepreneurial insight that allowed them to see the connection between broadcasting and print. Three years later he launched *Revelation* magazine, which by 1937 had a circulation of fifteen thousand. As the title indicates, with its reference to the last and perhaps most apocalyptic book of the Bible, Barnhouse was one more proponent of dispensationalist theology. The magazine gave him an outlet for commenting on developments in world affairs according to the script of biblical prophecy. But on a different level *Revelation* was important as one of many popular magazines circulated within the born-again subculture. Bible institutes such as Moody and BIOLA produced the *Moody Bible Institute Monthly* and *The King's Business*, respectively, as part of their effort to reach a wider audience.

The most popular of evangelical magazines to have a large circulation was the *Sunday School Times*, a weekly magazine published in Philadelphia and edited in the early twentieth century by Charles G. Trumbull. Founded in 1859, for the first sixty years of its existence this magazine was part of mainstream Protestantism and supported the work of the largest denominations. By the 1920s, however, Trumbull, a Presbyterian layman, had sided with conservatives against liberal Protestants. The *Times* then abandoned the institutions of mainline Protestantism in search of a readership that read the Bible without the assumptions of liberal theology. With a circulation of eighty thousand, the magazine functioned as born-again Protestantism's paper of record. Trumbull used its editorial pages as well as advertising to support trustworthy organizations, schools, and churches.

One sign of the shift in the *Times*'s orientation, as well as an indication of the way evangelical operations spawned other initiatives, was the weekly Sunday school lessons the magazine produced. They became a popular resource for churches that were suspicious of the educational literature coming out of the Protestant denominations' offices. The magazine had for many years published weekly "lesson helps" to assist Sunday school teachers who followed the International Sunday School Lesson Plans, a cooperative Protestant endeavor begun in the late nineteenth century to increase biblical literacy in the United States and even around the world. The idea was to have all Protestant churches following a similar Sunday school curriculum which would cover the Bible's contents over the course of a child's development and ensure uniformity of instruction no matter where children attended Sunday school. The *Times*'s lesson helps offered teachers tips on how to teach the assigned material. But once Trumbull identified the Protestant denominations as theologically bankrupt, the magazine abandoned the International Sunday School Lesson Plans format and offered its own curriculum.

The *Times* was not alone in this endeavor, and other publishing companies sprang up in response to the need among evangelicals for theologically safe educational material. The growth of evangelical publishing was predicated upon a growing sense that evangelicals were different not just from non-Christians but also from other Protestants, and so needed their own reading and educational material. Such publications may not have been read by those who subscribed to *Time* or

Life magazines, or who read the novels of Pearl Buck. But even though restricted to an earnestly devout segment of Protestantism, these publications helped create and sustain an identifiable religious subculture.

A final and important piece of the separate existence that evangelicals created in the wake of their estrangement from mainstream American society was the foreign missionary enterprise. Here born-again Protestants drew upon the past and at the same time introduced innovation. Throughout the nineteenth century American Protestantism had erected an expansive network for propagating Christianity and making converts in other parts of the world. By the end of the century the major Protestant denominations had added a variety of new activities, from education to medicine, in the belief that Christianity and the blessings of Western civilization went hand in hand. By the early decades of the twentieth century American Protestant churches were supporting close to twelve thousand missionaries in different parts of the world. The evangelical interest in missions continued this time-honored American Protestant conviction. Evangelicalism had historically stressed the importance of evangelism over the task of deepening the faith of those already converted. As such, the burgeoning of evangelical missions during the middle decades of the twentieth century tapped the spirit that had informed much of earlier American Protestant history.

At the same time evangelicals introduced a new twist on the missionary enterprise when, in response to their suspicion of the established Protestant denominations, they created and poured new energy into missions that were independent of and hence transcended any particular church or denomination. These "faith missions," as they were called, drew upon the sense of the imminent return of Christ that dispensationalist theology cultivated. Equipped with the conviction that the end of the world was near and that millions of souls were in need of the gospel, thousands of evangelicals enlisted with different missions agencies in hope of saving the lost. The two favorite agencies, both products of an earlier era, experienced renewed vigor in the decades after 1930. The China Inland Mission was a nondenominational agency that had begun in 1865 under British auspices and became prominent in the 1930s thanks to American evangelicals' enthusiasm and support. Between 1930 and 1936, even though China endured political turmoil, the China Inland Mission sent out 629 missionaries, many of them from the United States, almost doubling its number of workers. Another prominent missions agency independent of denominational sponsorship was the Sudan Interior Mission, an agency begun in 1893 by Protestants from Canada and the United States. A relatively small endeavor, this organization counted only 44 missionaries by 1920. But within a little more than two decades the missionary force of the Sudan Interior Mission had grown to 494 missionaries, thanks largely to the interest and zeal of evangelical Protestants in the United States.

Bible-institute and college graduates provided ready recruits for these agencies while the promise of serving in foreign missions instilled a sense of purpose and dedication throughout the evangelical subculture. At the same time that Bible colleges and institutes prepared future missionaries, evangelical magazines brought news of overseas work into the homes of American Protestants, and evangelical broadcasters encouraged listeners to support and consider the work of foreign missions. In a way, evangelical missions were the glue holding the movement together. Its missionaries were in the front lines of a religious battle between the forces of darkness and light; they were examples and heroes whose successes sustained evangelicals at home. The sacrifices sometimes re-

quired in the United States seemed inconsequential compared
to those in remote lands, and were thus ultimately worthwhile.

All of these institutions of the evangelical subculture signaled an important trend in American religion. One point
that is difficult to miss about the organizations, schools,
broadcasts, and publications into which evangelicals threw
their energy is that these institutions were independent of the
established and prosperous Protestant denominations in the
United States. Just as important to note, however, is that these
institutions depended very little on churches of any kind,
whether liberal or evangelical. The agencies that gave evangelicals a separate identity from the Protestant mainstream
transcended the work of local churches and denominations.
Often they enlisted support and provided encouragement to
born-again Christians no matter whether they were members,
for instance, of a United Methodist congregation or the local
fundamentalist Baptist church. In other words, the work of
institutional churches had little bearing on evangelical institutions because these agencies were performing activities that although religious were not narrowly churchly. They did not
involve directly the kinds of prayers, sermons, songs, and rites
in which Protestants participated when they gathered on Sundays for worship. One way of describing these institutions is to
call them "parachurch," meaning that they existed alongside
the church but were not the church proper. And one of the
hallmarks of twentieth-century American evangelicalism has
been its parachurch orientation. Whether owing to the controversies of the 1920s or to its revivalist heritage, evangelicals
have thrived outside churches and denominations in religious
organizations that are indifferent to the markings—creeds,
liturgy, and forms of church government—that distinguish
the various Protestant denominations, such as Baptists,

Lutherans, Congregationalists, Methodists, Episcopalians, and Presbyterians.

Another way of considering the institutional life of the evangelical subculture is to speak of these organizations as special-purpose groups. They exist alongside churches but concentrate on more specialized activities. American Protestantism has a long history of such institutions as tract and Bible societies or educational associations. But these special-purpose organizations did not simply exist alongside the churches; they began to compete with them for the religious identity of Protestants. For instance, in 1900 the ratio of denominations to special-purpose religious organizations was 2 to 1. By the end of World War II the ratio had narrowed to 1.2 to 1. The effect of this shift has meant that Protestant adherents in the twentieth century, especially evangelicals, are far more likely to identify themselves by the special-purpose groups in which they participate rather than by their church membership. Being a subscriber to *Moody Monthly* may be just as important for an evangelical as being a Lutheran might be for a nonevangelical. This shift of loyalty has occurred because evangelicals have frequently found more benefit in the broadcasts of their favorite radio preacher than in the sermons of their local minister.

Because of its orientation to parachurch agencies, evangelicalism during the first half of the twentieth century was fragmented according to the local networks established, for instance, by Bible schools, radio broadcasts, or foreign missions organizations. Dispensational theology helped keep these relatively isolated endeavors together through the zeal it generated for evangelizing unbelievers before the end of the world. But evangelicalism gained considerably more cohesion when an institution emerged whose aim was to give born-again Christians a collective and national identity.

This cohesion occurred in 1942 with the founding of the National Association of Evangelicals (NAE). Interestingly enough, the origins of this organization lay in one of the various local evangelical networks in which born-again Protestants flourished during the 1930s, in this case the New England Fellowship, a loose constellation of conferences, Bible colleges, religious broadcasts, and publications centered in Boston. The leader of this effort, J. Elwin Wright (1897–1986), believed that smaller evangelical organizations needed to affiliate with a larger group if they were to make a difference in American society. During the early 1940s Wright solicited the help of other evangelical leaders in promoting a national evangelical organization. In 1942, at the first annual conference of the association, held in St. Louis, Wright witnessed the fruit of his hard work. There attendees laid plans for a constitution and membership requirements while listening to inspirational speeches about the purpose of the organization. In Wright's own words, he wished to introduce among evangelicals a "new spirit of cooperation" and work toward a large-scale revival that would "sweep across our land like mighty showers of spiritual refreshing."

Although the NAE failed in the long run to become the center of evangelical action, it did succeed in introducing the evangelical label as the term of identity for born-again Protestants. Before the 1940s "evangelical" was a term in American religion that applied to all Protestants, except for Unitarians. For instance, when the largest Protestant denomination in 1908 formed the Federal Council of Churches (the very ecumenical body that born-again Protestants in the 1940s believed to have been captured by liberalism), practically all speakers at the council's first conference referred to the member churches as "evangelical Protestants" or "evangelical Christians." Even in the 1920s, such prominent liberal Protestants as the University of Chicago Divinity School's Shailer Mathews described the new theology as a scientific version of evangelical religion. What this designation meant before the 1940s was that such believers were good American Protestants, not Roman Catholics or members of a cult. But with the emergence of a national organization for evangelicals, the word became restricted to those Protestants who emphasized being born again, relied upon revivals as a way of gaining new converts, and read the Bible as a source of divine wisdom for all of life. Interestingly, the NAE did not limit membership to churches or denominations but also encouraged parachurch agencies as well as individuals to join. For this reason the NAE's founding represented a milestone in twentieth-century evangelicalism. Its very existence signaled the vitality and diversity of the evangelical institutions that had been formed since the 1920s to fill the vacuum created when born again Protestants became suspicious of the mainline denominations. The NAE also testified to the separate identity that the evangelical subculture had nurtured. Although local networks and enterprises would continue to be more important in the lives of ordinary evangelicals than membership in the NAE, the association demonstrated that the work of separation from mainstream society did not necessarily relegate evangelicals to oblivion.

The founding of new institutions, no matter how important in creating an evangelical identity, was by no means the only aspect of an alternative culture for born-again Protestants. What was perhaps just as important for the long-term survival of evangelicalism, and responsible for creating an audience for and donors to special-purpose religious organizations, was the evangelical family. In the home, parents sought to create an environment that would shield children from the harmful influences of secular society and instill the religious convictions necessary for a holy life set apart for Christian service. As much as a Bible college or radio broadcast might generate enthusiasm for a specific cause, the family was the place where evangelical ways and attitudes were learned and cultivated most directly.

Although evangelicals have received a fair amount of attention for what many perceive to be their peculiar views on the roles of husbands and wives in the home, just as important has been the evangelical understanding of the family and its role in child-rearing. Of all evangelical institutions, the family has been the most reliable. Even if the schools failed to instill proper values—which many evangelicals believed, thanks to evolution—and even if the churches abandoned their duty to preach faithfully, in the home evangelicals could find not simply a safe retreat but also sustenance for life in a hostile world. Two books of advice to evangelical families from the first half of the twentieth century illustrate the importance of the home for born-again Protestants as well as their expectations for its proper functioning.

In *The Home Beautiful*, originally published in the United States in 1912 and continuing in print into the 1930s, J. R. Miller provided evangelicals with a comprehensive perspective on home life, from the responsibilities of husbands and wives in their marriage vows all the way to the difficulties attending old age. The author's understanding of the home was simply that of a "place for growth"—where parents could "grow into beauty of character . . . in refinement, in knowledge, in strength, in wisdom, in patience, gentleness, kindliness, and all the Christian graces and virtues," and where children could also "grow into physical vigor and health." Perhaps the most revealing advice, however, concerned Miller's conception of how parents were to train their sons and daughters "in all that shall make them true and noble men and women." The desire of evangelical parents, according to Miller, should be "not merely to control them and keep them in order," but also to "implant true principles deep in their hearts which shall rule their whole lives." Put simply, parents should strive to train children, not simply govern them. Such training would result in children who honored their parents according to the Fifth Commandment by confiding in their mother and father, by learning self-denial, and by displaying thoughtfulness. Miller was lean on the specifics of how to in-still these principles; he was much better at describing the ideal home. But he did make clear that a heavy burden for rearing children of the right character fell upon mothers, since fathers who worked outside the home had fewer chances to exercise such training. In fact, Miller granted a holiness to the sphere of motherhood that bordered on excessive. "O mothers of young children," he wrote, "I bow before you in reverence . . . The powers folded up in the little ones that you hushed to sleep in your bosoms last night are powers that shall exist forever."

Although written almost three decades later, J. A. Huff-man's *Building the Christian Home* (1935) reiterated themes from Miller's earlier book while offering a few more specifics. The home, according to Huffman, was "the oldest and di-vinest of institutions," the place where "the child should be trained." Here children should "receive [their] precept and ex-ample, and here [they] should be carefully environed and faithfully disciplined." The home was so important in Huff-man's estimation that he could claim it to be the "foundation of church and state." Key to child training was precept. "Those in charge of the child should have carefully thought out and well-defined precepts, and should enunciate them considerately, lovingly, plainly and firmly." Parents also needed to live by their own precepts. Huffman wrote of a fa-ther who had discovered his thirteen-year-old son smoking, punished him for doing so, and threatened him with further punishment if he was found smoking again. But the father also smoked and therefore "had no moral right to punish his son for following his example." In effect, evangelical child training was a two-way street; its primary purpose was to train boys and girls with character, but indirectly it also required parents to internalize the same set of disciplines.

As oppressive as the evangelical home may have appeared from the outside, and as sentimental as evangelical writers may appear in their estimate of the family's importance, it is important to remember that many Americans regarded the home in similar terms. For instance, in his last chapter Huffman finished his argument not with a quotation from the Bible but rather from former President Calvin Coolidge:

> The home is the greatest influence in our natural life. Whatever may be done to make it better and more attractive is a real contribution to the nation as well as to the individual. We are told that some of the social, moral and spiritual problems of today are due in a measure to the disappearance of the old home life. It is our task to adjust the home to modern conditions so that it will continue to hold our children, teach them wholesome habits of living, and instill high ideals and the spirit of service.

Fears about wayward youth and concern for the powerful role of parents and the home in checking juvenile delinquency would continue to be themes of public discussions well into the decade after World War II. The evangelical outlook on the family clearly added religious elements that nonevangelicals may have rejected, such as when Huffman and Miller each insisted that instilling faith in boys and girls was crucial to the sort of character and virtues they promoted. Nonetheless evangelicals were not out of the mainstream in their emphasis on the home or the importance of the family to the smooth workings of American society.

As is already evident from Huffman's book, evangelical

parents were expected to follow and pass on a pattern of behavior that was different from that of non-Christians. Evangelical piety was premised on the conviction that conversion
transformed a person so thoroughly that he or she would no
longer engage in unholy or worldly activity. Parents were thus
encouraged not simply to read the Bible, pray, and attend
worship services with their children, aside from listening to
Christian radio broadcasts or subscribing to evangelical magazines; they also knew to avoid certain behaviors. Smoking, as
Huffman indicated, was one such evangelical taboo. Another
was alcohol. As J. Oliver Buswell, the president of Wheaton
College, located in the suburbs of Chicago, explained in his little book *The Christian Life* (1937), drunkenness was "the vor-
tex into which our young people are being swept by the
thousands, through the path of moderate drinking." He
played on fears of the slippery slope to conclude that Christians who drank moderately had to give up alcohol—even if
Christ himself turned water into wine at the wedding of
Cana—because by their example they led teens "into a life of
drunkenness." Although the most prominent, smoking and
drinking were not the only practices that defined evangelical
mores and informed their engagement with the wider culture.
Sexual chastity and modest attire; abstinence from cursing and
swearing, and from dancing, jazz, theater, movies, cards, and
gambling; and Sundays devoted to worship and rest were all
signs of evangelical piety. These rules were clearly enforced at
evangelical liberal arts and Bible colleges. Yet they were not
simply designed to reign in unruly youth and protect evangelical teens from the pressures of teen culture. They were also
an extension of the kind of ethic that evangelical parents established in the home. As restrictive and joyless as the evangelical way of life might have seemed, it is important to regard
it also as the badge of a particular Protestant faith. As such, its
practices—or in many cases, nonpractices—set evangelicals

apart from American society, giving them a separate identity both religiously and culturally.

Evangelicals were convinced that the kinds of amusements they avoided and the stern moral code that born-again parents exacted from their children were based upon the clear teachings of the Bible. Yet explanations from scriptural teaching were not as widespread as evangelical beliefs about the Bible would suggest. What is safe to say is that the Bible gave evangelicals a rallying point and a powerful marker of self-identity. It symbolized the authority of God and the supernaturalism of Christianity, the very ideas that mainline Protestants appeared to question. When it came to justifications for evangelical behavioral standards, a far greater influence was the "Keswick" movement, a specific branch of evangelical teaching that became popular in late-nineteenth-century Britain at a conference center in Keswick, England, and spread to North America, where it became the mainstay of evangelical reflection about Christian living during the twentieth century.

Keswick teaching focused on the believer's life after conversion and offered counsel on ways of becoming holier or more sanctified. Key to this movement was the notion, "Let go, let God." By surrendering themselves to God, Christians opened themselves up to being controlled by divine power. Keswick teaching could lead to preoccupation with the work of the Holy Spirit and efforts to experience God's presence fully or completely, as when Pentecostals made speaking in tongues (an unknown language) a badge of this extra form of divine blessing. But even if it did result in more demonstrable expressions of devotion, the Keswick teaching always stressed surrender. The way of faith was one of denying selfish desires and pleasures and living to please God in deeds of spiritual significance.

One illustration of the Keswick movement's influence

comes from the writing of Lewis Sperry Chafer, the founder of Dallas Theological Seminary, who helped make dispensationalism a mainstay of twentieth-century evangelical theology. In a book first published in 1918, *He That Is Spiritual,* Chafer showed how evangelicals could insist on being people of the book and yet offer few biblical specifics about the way Christians should behave. He wrote, "A Spiritual Christian is a Spirit-filled Christian in whom the unhindered Spirit is manifesting Christ by producing a true Christian character, which is the 'fruit of the spirit.'" What mattered, then, for truly godly living was being filled with divine influences, not following a list of rules and regulations. "How misleading," Chafer explained, "is the theory that to be spiritual one must abandon play, diversion and helpful amusement." Instead the path of obedience lay in being filled with God's presence, an experience that would remove desires for worldly pleasures and amusements and result in acts of sacrifice and service, and in a life yielded to the will of God. According to Chafer, the highest motive for yielding to God's will was to "live the sacrificial life which is the Christ life." Such sacrifice was not automatically painful, though "some pain may be in the path." But it was also a life of "joy" and "peace."

The irony of the Keswick teaching is that the apparent passivity it encouraged—being open to spiritual influences—became a vacuum that could be filled with rules, regulations, and expectations. Smoking, cards, dancing, movies—all such worldly amusements were prohibited not because the Bible said so explicitly but because they were believed to be barriers to the Spirit. This was the negative side of evangelical devotion. The positive side was a commitment to sacrificial service. In the same way that avoiding worldly pleasures became an index to true spirituality, so dedicating oneself to such "full-time Christian service" as foreign missions, preaching, or other religious enterprises also showed where a person's true

motives were and whether God was present in them. Even ordinary believers could demonstrate such sacrificial service by
witnessing to non-Christians on the job and by financially
supporting missionaries. The ideal of surrender and sacrifice
defined the evangelical subculture. Born-again Protestants
were cut off from the world and its amusements; they had created a set of institutions dedicated to saving the lost and to
generating support for that cause.

As much as evangelicals refrained from pleasures their
neighbors may have considered desirable, born-again Protestants were not averse to amusement. In his book on true spirituality even Chafer admitted, "It is a serious thing to remove
the element of relaxation and play from any life." Evangelicals
could not be "normal physically, mentally or spiritually" if
they neglected "this vital factor in human life." Consequently,
while evangelicals avoided worldly amusements they cultivated their own wholesome versions of fun, relaxation, and
recreation. Born-again parents, for example, did not simply
shut their children up at home and force them to memorize
large portions of the Bible. These parents also listened to religious broadcasts that provided a sanitized, but also slick, form
of evangelical entertainment. Their homes received the books
and magazines produced by evangelical publishing houses,
many of which included games and activities for youngsters
and stories and biographies for teens that filled the vacuum of
cultural withdrawal. Evangelicals also found ways of playing
card games that avoided gambling yet stoked the competitive
urges of the faithful. And many evangelical families even
found a way of turning the fun of vacation into a religious endeavor where the leading voices of the movement, whether on
the radio or from the area Bible college, would offer instruction and inspiration in a recreational and family-friendly environment.

Among the most prominent of these vacation spots was

Winona Lake Bible Conference, located in northern Indiana, just a short drive from Chicago. Reports on what transpired at this religious resort vary. Some emphasize its pedagogical character, with a program that offered as many as six sermons or lectures a day. Winona's speakers knew no denominational boundaries. They were united instead by a loyalty to the Bible and a desire to lead a holy life. The number of meetings at Winona indicated that evangelicals were serious and committed. Other reports on the proceedings list a wide assortment of leisure and recreational activities which show that evangelicals were not so serious as to avoid fun altogether. Swimming and boating, along with tennis and croquet, provided outlets for the more vigorous. Some weeks featured concerts, plays by Shakespeare, lectures on the evils of alcohol, and even performances by trained pets. Winona may have been exceptional among evangelical Bible conferences because of its late-nineteenth-century origins and its affiliation with the Chautauqua program of summer recreation and continuing education, but its ethos did not differ from such other evangelical camp-grounds as the Rumney Bible Conference in New Hampshire, the Boardwalk Bible Conference in Atlantic City, the Montrose Summer Conference in eastern Pennsylvania, Red-feather Lakes in Colorado, or Sandy Cove in Maryland. These camps and resorts offered evangelicals a safe retreat for inspiration and relaxation. They also provided a family-friendly atmosphere for parents with young children and young adults seeking escape from worldly temptations.

Bible conferences and camps like Winona sprang up between 1910 and 1940 and helped to define the convictions and leisure of evangelical Protestants. Their ability to attract whole families as well as college-age young people also spoke volumes about the movement. In many respects, by the middle decades of the twentieth century evangelical Protestantism was emerging as a young people's faith, both for families concerned about rearing children and for earnest young single adults committed to living a life uncompromised by what they saw as the emptiness and immorality of secular culture. In one sense this demographic reality was predictable. The new institutions and churches that evangelicals formed after the fundamentalist controversy were much more likely to attract young adults, people starting out in life who had less at stake in the established organizations and parishes of mainline Protestantism. In another sense, evangelicalism appealed to young people, teens and adults, because its message of deciding for Christ coincided with that stage in life when young men and women, parents and single, were choosing an identity for themselves rather than relying on inherited patterns of religious adherence.

Indicative of evangelicalism's youthful orientation was the emergence in 1945 of Youth for Christ, an organization that consolidated the work of a variety of urban youth ministries across the United States. The leaders of these endeavors assembled at the Winona Lake Bible Conference to found an international organization whose purpose was to sponsor rallies in metropolitan centers for America's teenagers.

Well before 1945, evangelical interest in youth ministry had sprung up as part of local congregations' efforts to shelter and reach teenagers. In such cities as New York, Boston, Philadelphia, Detroit, and Chicago, evangelical churches cultivated leaders who possessed entrepreneurial energy and were not afraid to couch Protestantism in the idiom of popular culture. Many of these men's names are not well remembered, but they were pivotal in cultivating a generation of Protestants that sustained the evangelical subculture. A large part of their appeal was to make it fun to be an evangelical. In a book written for youth ministers, *Reaching Youth for Christ* (1945), Torrey Johnson, a Midwestern pastor, and Robert Cook, an evangelist, offered advice on how to make the faith once delivered to the saints relevant and, above all, upbeat. Young people had grown accustomed to Hollywood production standards and commercial radio and so would automatically "shun" meetings that were shoddily staged and promoted. Thus effective ministry to teens required the timing of the best comedy, peppy gospel music, references to current events, moving testimonials from converts—in other words, a good show. In these youth rallies music was a powerful draw. Just as was the case with radio evangelists, a cadre of entertainers and popular songs emerged that were the evangelical counterpart to the popular music and entertainment stars of the era. Evangelical youth pastors and musicians also broke with the staid attire of the minister and wore pastel-colored suits, sometimes accompanied by bow ties or hand-painted neckties, which raised the eyebrows of some who thought flashiness and Christianity were incompatible. So successful was the evangelical outreach to teens that throughout the summer of 1945 crowds of young people flocked to Chicago's Orchestra Hall to hear gospel music and energetic evangelists. The high point of this effort was a "Victory Rally" which filled to capacity Chicago's Soldier Field. The size of such meetings could hardly go unnoticed. But the rallies themselves also generated goodwill from civic leaders who worried about the morality of America's youth.

Aside from numerical success and good publicity, the most important development in evangelicalism's youth ministry was its development of an evangelical superstar who would become the defining figure of twentieth-century born-again Protestantism. The first speaker at Chicago's summer youth rallies of 1945 was Billy Graham (1918–), a relatively unknown pastor from the surrounding suburbs. Through such speaking engagements, Graham came to the attention of leaders within evangelical youth ministry. Once the organization that linked the various local youth initiatives together, Youth for Christ, was established that same year, Graham found a platform that would give him national exposure. By 1946 he was Youth for Christ's principal speaker, traveling to forty-seven states and gaining the notoriety of being United Airlines' most frequent civilian passenger. The following year Youth for Christ sent Graham to Great Britain for a series of crusades in which he spoke at 360 meetings over a period of six months. Historians have acknowledged that Graham was not the most polished of the young evangelicals committed to winning America's teens. He had studied at Wheaton College in Illinois and at Bob Jones University but took his speaking style directly from radio preachers he had listened to as a boy in rural North Carolina. What accounted for Graham's success even more than his patterns of speech, as his more talented peers recognized, were his good looks, charisma, and lack of pretension, which seemed to connect immediately with audiences.

Even so, Graham did not enter the national spotlight until September 1949. Through the orchestration of a team of evangelists who were concentrating their efforts on Southern California, he arrived in Los Angeles that month to conduct a citywide revival. It had all the features of a Youth for Christ rally. The organizers had used publicity techniques honed by Youth for Christ, and Graham's meetings combined the music of George Beverly Shea with preaching aimed at contemporary problems. On the list of matters that generated Graham's and his listeners' alarm were the threat of nuclear war, urban crime, and a general increase in immortality and godlessness throughout American society. Graham also spoke frequently about the health of the American family. Despite a new level of earnestness in his delivery, after three weeks crowds to the meetings began to flag. But then the unexpected happened. A local radio celebrity, Stuart Hamblen, converted and began to urge listeners to attend the rallies. Hamblen's interest soon attracted the attention of William Randolph Hearst, the fabled newspaper magnate, who urged his reporters and editors to "puff Graham." The unanticipated publicity turned what looked like a fairly mediocre revival into the launching pad for Billy Graham's exceptional career as the poster boy for twentieth-century evangelicalism.

As much as the events that transpired in Los Angeles during the fall of 1949 pointed toward a brighter future for evangelicalism, they also built upon developments in the movement's not-so-distant past. Born-again Protestants flourished between 1930 and 1950 by building separate religious institutions, many of which contravened the conventional workings of the church. In the process they created a spiritual subculture geared toward families, teens, and young adults. In many respects evangelical piety demanded an emphasis on young people because of its conviction that entrance into the faith required the fully free decision of the sovereign individual. The church and home could do only so much. Evangelicalism required individuals who had come to see the truth of the gospel for themselves. The genius of evangelicalism has been to create organizations that, although designed to protect the faithful from a hostile world, also grant individuals the opportunity to experience religion free from guidance or predisposition. What is more, evangelicals thrived during these years because of their ability to package Christianity in a popular—some might say crude—idiom or style. Ever since the early nineteenth century, evangelicalism grew precisely because of its populist appeal. During the late nineteenth century, as the mainstream denominations became stronger organizationally, the churches bottled up much of revivalism's vigor. But once free from the churches, thanks to the fundamentalist controversy, the evangelicals of Billy Graham's generation rediscovered their religion's unique blend of gospel zeal and practical know-how, which in turn produced a subculture that was to insiders as fun-loving and vigorous as to outsiders it appeared humorless and severe.

A large irony attended Billy Graham's hugely successful Los Angeles crusade of 1949. A movement that in the 1920s had withdrawn from the privileged position of the mainstream Protestant churches and established separate institutions in order to preserve the true faith, by 1950 had become a na-tional—even international—phenomenon that was beginning to occupy its own respectable space in mainstream American culture. Indeed, the reversal of evangelicalism's fortunes from 1925, just after the Scopes Trial, to 1950, when Graham was beginning to become a household name, is truly remarkable. In many respects this shift from cultural outsider to respected member of American society is the typical route of many eth-nic groups throughout United States history. After first estab-lishing separate institutions and culture, most immigrants have then used these associations and neighborhoods to enter the wider culture and assimilate American ways. Historians have often compared the twentieth-century evangelical expe-rience to that of an ethnic group with its own culture, lan-guage, and institutions. In the case of the evangelicals, their subculture did in fact provide a foundation for the move-ment's eventual emergence after 1950 as a force in American society.

But as useful as the immigrant analogy may be, it is still only an analogy. Born-again Protestants, though feeling alien-ated, were among the most American of Americans. Most were not recent immigrants from other lands. They spoke En-glish and were steeped in American notions about individual-ism, autonomy, and equality. What is more, the United States was for many evangelicals their homeland and enjoyed a unique status in God's plan for world history. The reason evangelicals rejected the cultural patterns in which other

Protestants moved was not ethnic but spiritual; born-again Protestants were deeply ambivalent about the ways of the world because of their beliefs about the fallenness of things earthly and the need for divine intervention to make human endeavors holy. This was perhaps the greatest factor fueling the creation of a separate evangelical subculture—the hope of establishing a world untainted by human hands, where the Spirit would move freely and believers would be preserved pure and undefiled. What evangelicals did not adequately consider was that the energy of their human hands would generate large and successful earthly organizations whose leaders displayed impressive organizational savvy. That may be the biggest irony of all.

3

Evangelicals and the Politics of Morality

ONE OF THE REASONS that Billy Graham attracted support from the likes of William Randolph Hearst was that the evangelist's politics were decidedly sympathetic to those who championed big business and America's supremacy in world affairs. Political conservatives in the United States might not have phrased it in the religious terms that Graham used, but when he described communism as a form of tyranny "masterminded by Satan," many Americans not only got the point but agreed. And when Graham spoke of the United States as "the key nation of the world," "the last bulwark of Christian Civilization," he also touched a nerve. Since just after World War II, when America entered the cold war with the Soviet Union, many American leaders had pointed to the nation's special responsibility for saving the West from the onslaught of despotism and repression. Indeed, Graham's early success can be explained in part by the trick he and other youth pastors had learned of making Christianity relevant to contemporary social problems. Consequently a decision to follow Christ at one of Graham's crusades also conveyed political and national benefits, as the evangelist described them in his sermon "Satan's Religion." The five most effective ways of fighting communism, he declared, were, first, "old-fashioned

Americanism"; second, "conservative and Evangelical Christianity"; third, "prayer"; fourth, "a genuine spiritual revival"; and finally, "personal Christianity."

The ease with which Graham could speak about affairs that were explicitly political in rallies that were supposed to be spiritual may have appeared odd to secular observers. But it was a natural occurrence within evangelicalism, thanks to born-again Protestantism's practical orientation. Ever since the eighteenth-century revivals of the First Great Awakening, evangelicals have affirmed that one of the marks of genuine faith is personal and social morality. This is not to say that other Christians, both Catholic and Protestant, hold that believers may be morally bankrupt and still be good Christians. But unlike other forms of Christianity where the understanding of faith includes a life beset by struggles with temptation and sin, evangelicals have insisted that, despite these trials, believers must overcome such tests and live victorious lives where upright behavior is evident for all to see. This close link between conversion and moral perfection has been at the root of evangelical attitudes toward the relationship between faith and society, or between religion and politics. A truly righteous nation, according to evangelical logic, will be one where most of the people have a personal relationship with Jesus Christ. For this reason, for evangelicals the solution to many social and political problems is nothing less than conversion and faith.

Graham illustrated the relevance of revivalism for America's social well-being when he preached on the problem of juvenile delinquency. One of the aspects of 1950s society that bedeviled many observers was the apparent discrepancy between the revival of religion—for which Graham himself deserved credit—and escalating rates of teenage crime. The revivalist's explanation drew heavily from evangelicalism's supernaturalistic worldview. "The Bible teaches," Graham declared, "that we are engaged in a gigantic spiritual warfare, and when God begins to move in a country, as he is now moving mightily in America, Satan also begins to move." The import of religion for public welfare extended to other areas of politics as well. As such, Graham could also be heard in his evangelistic crusades denouncing Washington's deficit spending, the United Nations' meddling in the Korean War, the "evils" of big government and big labor, and even America's foreign aid policy. So ingrained in the evangelical mind was the idea that true religion yielded a well-ordered and righteous society (consisting of upright individuals) that few of Graham's supporters, staff, or listeners wondered about the propriety of mixing religion and politics, or whether faith always had such positive effects.

Whatever the shortcomings of evangelical approaches to politics, an interest in government and public affairs was not hard to find among born-again Protestants. Contrary to the notion that evangelicals were so preoccupied with the eternal destiny of souls that they neglected social or national affairs, the record shows that evangelicals were in fact sensitive to the political questions of the day. To be sure, their beliefs and convictions prompted an approach to public life that was different from their Protestant cousins in the mainline denominations. Nonetheless evangelicals retained an older American Protestant sense of responsibility for the welfare of the nation and brought their religion to bear upon political matters. Their political orientation owed much to the evangelical conviction that religion, if it were truly spiritual, inevitably shaped the behavior of citizens and ordered the affairs of nations.

At the beginning of the twentieth century the political views of evangelicals were scarcely different from the approach to government and civic affairs of most English-speaking Protestants in the United States. As they emerged from the

political and military contests of the Civil War, American
Protestants continued to be divided along sectional lines.
Evangelicals in the South voted primarily Democratic while
their fellow adherents in the North still backed the party of
Abraham Lincoln. But despite the different policies espoused
by Republicans and Democrats, along with the occasional
third party, born-again Protestants approached public life
from a common set of convictions. And just as evangelical religion transcended denominational beliefs and practices, so
born-again understandings of personal responsibility and social order usually trumped political party allegiances.

Evangelicals started from the conversionist premise that
genuine religion results in moral transformation, first of individuals and then of societies. They wanted ethical change that
avoided all forms of worldliness and resulted in a life of evangelistic outreach and spiritual zeal. This perspective yielded
two important implications for the evangelical view of politics. The first was a commitment to changing individuals first
through revivals and evangelism. Once a sufficient portion of
society had dedicated themselves to Christ, social structures
and government would see genuine change. The other impli-
cation of evangelical piety for politics was that it predisposed
born-again Protestants to view public life chiefly through
moral categories. Not only did they tend to become active politically on the basis of certain moral crusades, but their understanding of public life tended to lack nuance or compromise.
Political issues were either right or wrong, good or evil. This
set up winner-take-all outcomes which, when evangelicals
found themselves on the losing side, left little room for further
participation in the process.

Another important factor in evangelical politics was a high
estimate of the United States as a Christian nation. This understanding of America was partly based on the assumption
that religion was crucial to social order. The stability and

greatness of a society was linked inexorably to the moral health of its citizens, and morality had no proper foundation without faith. For American Protestants, this logic inevitably pointed to evangelicalism as the basis for the nation's greatness and progress. America's dependence on evangelical Protestantism also stemmed from born-again Protestant beliefs about the special role of their nation in God's plan of salvation. Stemming partly from older Puritan ideas about the New World functioning as a beacon of truth to the world, and partly from Protestant estimates of the American Revolution as a vindication of evangelical religion (as opposed to the tyranny of the Church of England and Roman Catholicism), born-again Protestants held the United States to a standard comparable to that used to evaluate the church. They could talk openly of America's religious fidelity in good times and the nation's apostasy in times of woe. This notion of the United States' religious identity and mission only reinforced the evangelical tendency to evaluate politics in moral categories, and it also contributed to a form of xenophobia. Evangelicals tended to be suspicious of believers whose religion was different from theirs, especially non-Protestants, and so regarded foreign influences as a threat to the nation's health.

The Protestants who emerged during the middle decades of the twentieth century as the bearers of the evangelical tradition have generally had the reputation of opposing the Social Gospel. This effort to apply Christianity to the nation's social crisis following the impact of industrialization, urbanization, and immigration in the late nineteenth century became a major initiative of the largest Protestant denominations in the first decade of the twentieth. The formation of the Federal Council of Churches in 1908 is one specific manifestation of American Protestants pursuing greater cooperation for the purpose of speaking with a unified voice to the social ills of

America. Because the Social Gospel, narrowly defined, included efforts to reform social, political, and economic structures, as opposed to simply trying to change individuals, historians have concluded that it was not congenial to evangelicals. To be sure, born-again Protestants placed little hope in changing people by reforming institutions; if forced to choose they always chose personal instead of social reform as most consistent with Christianity. Nevertheless this distinction between a social and an individual gospel was rarely cast as an either-or proposition. Moreover, evangelicals themselves supported many of the same reforms advocated by leaders of the Social Gospel.

For example, the two most prominent revivalists of the late nineteenth and early twentieth centuries, Dwight L. Moody (1837–1899) and Billy Sunday (1862–1935) were not proponents of the Social Gospel, but their own attitudes toward religion and society dovetailed in important respects with those who advocated a more prominent church role in social reform. Both revivalists opposed liquor and those who profited from its sale and distribution. They also championed a series of ethical standards, though perhaps more middle-class than biblical, that helped preserve the dominance of Anglo-American Protestants in the United States. Undoubtedly Moody and Sunday would have opposed any approach to evangelism that placed social reform ahead of soul-winning. But their applications of the gospel to society, considered simply on their own terms, differed little from the aims for preserving a Christian society proposed by the Federal Council of Churches. Only after the fundamentalist controversy did a choice between reform and evangelism seem to be required, with liberal Protestants advocating the former and evangelicals defending the latter. Even so, evangelicals did not oppose the kind of American society the Social Gospel promised, because the reforms promoted by the churches so closely reflected a morality indebted to born-again Protestantism. The differences were chiefly over means, not ends.

By the early twentieth century, then, evangelicals could be found mixing religious convictions with social interest. This did not necessarily result in a preference for the Democrats or the Republicans but did involve a definite idea of what was best for America as a nation. This evangelical political outlook included the following constellation of ideas:

—The Bible is the infallible rule for faith and practice, including standards of social justice and public morality.

—The United States possesses a special and unique role in the history of salvation, and so its conduct and affairs should conform to those reserved for the kingdom of God.

—The truths of Christianity, and especially the Protestant faith, provide the certain means for the spread of Western Civilization, both at home through the work of the churches and abroad through the efforts of missionaries.

—The Roman Catholic Church is a menace to democracy and the welfare of the United States because it is based upon ignorance, bigotry, and superstition.

These ideals were not distinctly evangelical but were circulated widely throughout the largest Protestant denominations. Together they proved to be an important motive for many of the social reforms and legislative initiatives of the Progressive Era. Yet born-again Protestants held on to this social outlook longer than their peers in the mainline churches.

One way of illustrating how evangelical perceptions of religion and public morality informed specific matters of policy is to notice the wholehearted support that born-again Protestants gave to two initiatives that were also dear to Anglo-American Protestantism at large—Prohibition and public education. On Prohibition, their stance reflected and reinforced nineteenth-century ideas about individual productivity, work, efficiency, and economic expansion that had funneled Northern evangelicals into the Republican party at the time of its founding. Alcohol symbolized for most English-speaking Protestants a form of tyranny that destroyed self-discipline and self-control, two virtues that also happened to benefit the United States' early industrial expansion; sober workers were reliable workers. In contrast, the issue of public education tapped evangelical notions about America not as individuals but as a corporate whole. For English-speaking Protestants, evangelicals included, public schools were the principal means of assimilating immigrants into American life. A crucial element in this conception was that the nation remain Christian and therefore Protestant. Public schools were conduits for Protestantism at least through the prayer and Bible reading that began most school days.

Evangelicals were not unique in their opposition to alcohol. During the first half of the nineteenth century many observers of American society became alarmed by the large quantities of drink that citizens consumed over the course of a day. Protestants founded temperance societies to promote moderate consumption. But by the late nineteenth century, when women's groups such as the Women's Christian Temperance Union entered the fray, abstinence, or total avoidance of alcohol, had become the rule for most Protestants. By the early twentieth century, when the temperance movement had become powerful enough to amend the Constitution with legislation banning the sale and distribution of alcohol, drink no longer stood simply for the dangers posed to free, responsible, and disciplined citizens but also for the tip of an iceberg of urban vice. In the minds of many Protestants, many of whom were decent, hardworking folk with a strict way of life, drinking involved more than the inevitable drunkenness or alcoholism that accompanied it; it was also the hub for a variety of lewd and lascivious behaviors, from gambling and prostitution to burlesque and vaudeville.

This perspective on alcohol and the surrounding culture of urban vice is important for understanding evangelical attitudes toward public affairs. An aspect of born-again Protestantism seldom remembered is how many prominent evangelical pastors during the first quarter of the twentieth century were actively involved not simply in trying to save souls but also in urban reform. Two notable examples are William Bell Riley, the Minneapolis Baptist pastor, and Mark A. Matthews (1867–1940), a Presbyterian minister in Seattle. Both men entered the turbulent waters of big-city politics with a gusto that evangelicals in the late twentieth century would only be able to muster for national and especially presidential politics. Their reformist activism did not qualify as the Social Gospel proper. But like that more liberal expression of Protestant involvement in public life, it sprung from evangelical ethical norms buried deep within the American Protestant soul. In both cases the underlying outlook was remarkably similar: social order depends on personal morality, and personal morality in the end depends on true religion. Political problems are finally spiritual or religious problems.

A native of southern Indiana, in 1897 Riley took a call to the First Baptist Church of Minneapolis, where he would remain for the rest of his life. He made an immediate splash in local politics when he preached a series of sermons on urban reform, eventually published as *Messages for the Metropolis* (1906). "The future of your city," he declared in terms that equally applied to the nation, "depends upon how many may be numbered among the redeemed of the Lord." Of course, if all citizens were saved, there would be no need for government. This is why for those who would not become Christians, the "enforced morality" of the government was necessary. The trouble was, in Riley's case, that city officials had not fulfilled their duty to rid Minneapolis of vice. Consequently, just as he had in previous pastorates, first in Bloomington, Indiana, and then in Chicago, Riley organized associations of citizens in pursuit of urban reform. Chief among the vices that plagued America's cities was liquor—in Riley's own words, the "mother" of all corruption. "The darkest blight on the municipal body," he asserted, "is that blood-stained institution you call the saloon." It would do the opposite of true religion; it would "convert the fairest child that ever drew sustenance from a mother's breast into the foulest fiend that ever fattened its lust upon the lives of others." Thanks to pressure from Riley, other ministers, and a civic federation that Riley helped to found, Minneapolis officials began to enforce laws that restricted saloon hours. Although Riley's religious convictions during the 1920s appeared backward to many intellectuals and journalists, his involvement in urban reform fit squarely in the mold of progressive politics and thus looked enlightened.

The case of Mark A. Matthews in Seattle was similar to that of Riley's. After two short pastorates in Georgia and Tennessee, where Matthews entered the field of politics, even to the point of studying law and becoming a member of the bar, he received a call to Seattle. There he immediately used his church as a bully pulpit for ridding the city of vice. According to Matthews, it was "the business of the Christian to be active in society, in business, in the domestic world and in the political sphere." He believed that "the bad citizenship of good citizens" was a greater danger than "bad citizens." Matthews applied this logic after just a few weeks in Seattle, accusing the city council of graft. Eventually he linked the mayor and other city officials to bribes from mobsters and those responsible for local prostitution and gambling establishments. So successful were Matthews's efforts that with the help of the women's vote he led the recall of Seattle's mayor. But as much as gambling and prostitution gained his attention, liquor was for Matthews, as for Riley, "the most fiendish, corrupt and hell-soaked institution that ever crawled out of the slime of the eternal pit." This was the basis for his support for Prohibition. Even though Matthews was less successful in blocking the liquor traffic, he did recognize that laws were insufficient in themselves for changing behavior. Consequently he proposed the establishment of coffeehouses and a city-sponsored recreation center as a substitute for saloons and bars.

While Matthews's and Riley's opposition to beverage alcohol found its primary outlet in the progressive politics of urban reform, William Jennings Bryan illustrates the application of evangelical views on liquor to national politics. Like other evangelicals, Bryan was opposed on religious grounds to alcohol consumption. Even during his tenure as secretary of state in the Wilson administration, stories circulated that Bryan and his wife would entertain public officials and serve grape juice instead of wine at sumptuous meals. But as a politician, Bryan also had to count the costs of involvement in the temperance crusade. For instance, when he ran in 1908 for the third time as the Democratic candidate for president of the United States, Bryan skirted the issue in order to avoid offending the distilling and brewing interests, a base of Democratic support. By the late 1910s, however, he had no hesitation throwing his support behind an amendment to the Constitution that would prohibit the sale and distribution of alcohol. In 1918, under the auspices of the Women's Christian Temperance Union, Bryan stumped in more than half the states of the Union and lobbied the Anti-Saloon League to win support for Prohibition. And later that year he was elected president of the National Dry Federation, an organization that included the Federal Council of Churches. So committed was Bryan to the cause that party loyalty did not matter. As he told audiences in the spring of 1918, a Republican who would vote in support of the constitutional amendment was better than a "WET" Democrat.

Bryan's willingness to see votes go to his former foes in the Republican party suggests the kind of single-issue perspective that evangelicalism has often interjected into public debates. Here the righteousness of the cause was so obvious that other national issues or principles of political philosophy must not interfere. Bryan himself demonstrated how a concern for holy living, both personally and collectively, could outweigh larger political considerations when he tried to explain how Prohibition legislation nonetheless conformed with the American ideals of liberty and limited government. In 1918 he wrote:

> Thousands, tens of thousands, hundreds of thousands of men who will vote against prohibition and who will think we are violating their personal rights will, when they are released from the habit and relieved from temptation, go down on their knees and thank us for having helped them against their will, and their wives and children will not have to wait a year; they will thank us now for saving their husbands and fathers.

In other words, the achievement of a dry nation, in which the temptation of strong drink no longer existed, justified narrowing the range of personal liberties. For evangelicals, when it came to public policy, religious categories often trumped conceptions of power, authority, economic interest, and freedom, whether local or national.

A similar logic attended the manner in which evangelicals viewed public schools and the function of public education. Ever since the founding of the American republic, English-speaking Protestants believed, as did the nation's political elites, that democracy's well-being depended upon a moral and upright citizenry. For deists like George Washington or

Thomas Jefferson, the simple ethical teachings of Jesus, such as the Golden Rule, were sufficient for nurturing the virtue essential to national well-being. This is why leaders such as Jefferson and James Madison, even though suspicious of excessive religious fervor, favored strong and effective churches. In the early nineteenth century, evangelicals responded to the nation's needs with a version of Christianity well suited to public life. Under the influence of Scottish philosophy, most Protestant churches embraced a theory of ethics which taught that everyone, whether Christian or not, could know intuitively the difference between right and wrong. In so doing, American Protestants came to hold that Christian morality was not only compatible with liberty and democracy; it was also the logical outcome of all right-thinking people. Because of Protestantism's close identification with American political ideals, it emerged as the unofficial religion of the United States. After the Revolution, several states continued to support Protestant churches through taxation on the premise that civil society needed a common and authoritative morality.

As the practices of established churches became more difficult to administer, the public school replaced the church as the institution best suited to instill the moral guidelines on which the United States depended. Not surprisingly, Protestants had a virtual monopoly on schooling in early America. This dominance extended even to the first public or "common" schools, where the curriculum consisted of Bible reading, prayers, hymn singing, and Protestant instructional materials. The reason for what would by the late twentieth century be a flagrant violation of the separation of church and state was the assumption by most Americans that Protestantism went hand in hand with political liberty. Of course, once Roman Catholics began to emigrate to the United States in large numbers, the Protestant bias of American public schooling became more obvious. And as a result, in large metropolitan areas such as New York City and Cincinnati, Roman Catholic clergy squared off with public school officials in an effort to secure funding for parochial schools. City politicians generally refused because they believed Roman Catholicism was too sectarian to benefit the public good. The compromise in these disputes invariably involved a reduction in the overtly Protestant content of public school exercises. Even so, by the late nineteenth century and the first decades of the twentieth century, when states began to make primary education mandatory, public schools retained a Protestant ethos owing to the opening-day exercises of prayer and Bible reading. According to surveys conducted in 1896 and 1903 by the U.S. Commission of Education, 75 percent of America's major urban school districts began the school day with Bible reading and prayer. In 1950 one student of church-state relations estimated that between 33 and 50 percent of the nation's schools still opened with religious exercises.

The Protestant orientation of America's public schools is important for understanding the evangelical perspective on American public life. Until the controversy over Darwinism, evangelicals had no real objection to the character of public education, not only because it was friendly to their religious convictions but because born-again Protestants believed in the historic mission of public schools, which was to instill a common morality. Especially during the period of the greatest influx of immigrants to the United States, the public schools, in the minds of many Protestants, bore the responsibility of assimilating non-Americans to American ways. As the author of *The Schooling of the Immigrant* (1920) perhaps indelicately put it, the nation looked "with anxious hope to the school as the chief instrument of Americanization." This social part of the public school's mission was plausible when it came to teaching reading and writing in English, along with some familiarity with American history and customs. But when this program also involved sending the message to immigrants that part of being a good American involved abandoning strange and foreign religions such as Catholicism and Judaism, public schools crossed the line between the duties of public life and parental efforts in the home. Yet because the underlying assumption of public education was that America was culturally a Protestant land and that the morality of Protestants was necessary for the nation's health, evangelicals could without hesitation endorse the mission of public schooling.

Protestant investment in public schooling helps explain why Darwinism became such a contentious issue during the 1920s. The most heated debates over evolution occurred not in church assemblies or theological journals but in the context of state laws governing the curriculum of public schools. William Jennings Bryan, who led the attack against evolution in public education, blended the utilitarian purpose of common schooling with the nation's need for moral guidelines. Reason, for Bryan, was a fickle instrument unless harnessed by spiritual and moral training. "A trained mind," he explained, "can add largely to the usefulness of life when it is under the control of the spiritual in man, but it can wreck any human being, even civilization itself, if it is allowed to exercise authority." For this reason, schools needed to impart moral truths rooted in faith if they were to succeed in their mission of engineering a righteous society. Germany's aggression during World War I only proved to Bryan the consequences of a high esteem for science and education unchecked by religious truths and morality. From his perspective, the world needed love and could only find it in Christ. "Love makes money-grabbing contemptible; love makes class prejudices impossible; love makes selfish ambition a thing to be despised." The problem with evolution in public schools, then, was not that it was untrue. According to Bryan, "the principle objection to evolution is that it is highly harmful to those who accept it." Allowing evolution to be taught in public schools—institutions whose mission had included inculcating Protestantism's spiritual and religious ideals—would ruin the United States.

Bryan's views on public education were not simply religious. They also stemmed from notions about majority rule and the rights of the people to determine public policy. Even so, the religious part of his approach to public schooling indicated how evangelicals have looked at American politics. As in the case of alcoholic beverages, born-again Protestants started with certain ethical convictions about the nature of a righteous or holy society, and evaluated institutions or policies according to whether they advanced a Christian way of life. Thus political philosophy mattered less than spiritual welfare. The United States provided enough proof of the positive effects of Protestantism upon public life. America was the freest, most prosperous, and strongest nation in the world, and its religious basis was largely responsible. This is why for evangelicals the moral welfare of the nation could not be separated from the spiritual health of individuals. The saving of souls inevitably resulted in the salvation of societies.

Until the second quarter of the twentieth century, the political differences between evangelical and mainline Protestants were hard to come by. As the historian Mark A. Noll helpfully concludes:

> Protestants in the progressive era relied instinctively on the Bible to provide their ideals of justice. They believed in the power of Christ to expand the Kingdom of God through the efforts of faithful believers. They were reformists at home and missionaries abroad who felt that cooperation among Protestants signaled the advance of civilization. They were thoroughly and uncritically patriotic.

The reasons for these similarities stem partly from a common understanding of Christianity where theology mattered less than the practical outworking of faith in individual lives. As much as fundamentalists and liberals may have disagreed about the virgin birth of Christ, both were agreed on the kind of morality prescribed in the Bible for individuals and nations. What is more, evangelical and mainline Protestants shared a similar estimate of the United States' importance in the history of salvation, even if they disagreed about the specifics of how individuals were saved. In other words, the ecclesiastical controversies of the 1920s that helped create evangelicalism as a category separate from the Protestant mainstream did not fundamentally alter English-speaking Protestants understanding of the relationship between religion and society.

The one aspect, however, that did set evangelical political interests apart from those of their mainline cousins was the theological system of dispensationalism. It fueled the array of institutions that gave a separate identity to born-again Protestants. Because of dispensationalism's preoccupation with Bible passages dealing with end times and the second coming of Christ, and because many of these portions of Scripture addressed conflicts between Israel and other nations, this method of interpreting the Bible nurtured an interest in international politics that could become almost manic in times of war, natural catastrophes, or changes in political leadership. Evangelicals believed they were living in the last days, and the Bible gave them clues about how near the end was. As such, dispensationalism produced among evangelicals a strange political brew. In domestic affairs it appealed to well-worn Protestant notions about American society, but in international politics it spoke with an apocalyptic accent.

Yet no matter how bizarre their interpretation of foreign politics may have appeared to those unaccustomed to dispensationalism's theology, born-again Protestants remained committed to the common sense of American politics. This feature of evangelical political reflection was particularly evident in the preoccupation that born-again leaders exhibited toward fascism and communism. During the years from World War I to the cold war, evangelicals could engage in endless speculation about the doings of a Mussolini, Hitler, or Stalin. But underneath the slang and code words of dispensationalist theology about the dangers of authoritarianism was the fundamental aversion of American political ideals to tyranny in practically any form.

World War I and its aftermath, just as it had for the church controversies, proved pivotal in spurring evangelicals to apply dispensationalist theology to world affairs. On the one hand, the capturing of Jerusalem in 1917 by the British, and the ensuing pledge of a national homeland for Jews in Palestine, excited evangelical speculation about reconstituting the nation of Israel—always an important component of biblical prophecy about Christ's return. On the other hand, the Russian Revolution in 1917 stoked a common evangelical fear that Russia would fulfill the Bible's prophecy about a godless people from the north who would invade the Middle East and unleash Armageddon. The rise of dictators in Italy and Germany in the late 1920s and early 1930s provoked further speculation about international politics. Benito Mussolini's emergence in Italy appeared to he especially relevant to the Bible's teaching that in the last times the former Roman Empire would reunite. But Adolf Hitler's designs for Germany proved to be harder for evangelicals to fathom since that nation—partly because it gave birth to the Protestant Reformation—had not figured prominently in the wicked designs of nations that would mark the end of the world. Still, Hitler's emergence as a dictator par excellence provided sufficient material for evangelicals to compare him to the Antichrist who would dominate the world just before the last stage of human and salvation history.

Dispensationalism also reinforced evangelicals' perceptions of domestic affairs and confirmed their socioeconomic preferences. Although the Great Depression was a source of suffering for many evangelicals, the economic woes prompted an attitude of vindication from many of the movement's leaders. Here finally was proof, contrary to the optimistic theology of liberal Protestants, that the world situation was growing worse, not better, and that evangelicals had been right in their diagnosis of society all along. As one North Carolina preacher put it, "Some are beginning to discover that the faith of our fathers is not the back-number proposition some sophomore smart alecks thought it was." Or as another explained, for many years the intellectuals had spent most of their time "boasting of man's high attainments upon the earth, his high degree of civilization, his great advancement," but now they were talking in "whispers of fear." At the same time the depression gave evangelicals a measure of satisfaction in their former prognosis, attempts to ameliorate the situation through the New Deal stimulated greater attention to the possibilities of totalitarianism at home. Some evangelicals were prompted to compare America's dictatorial ways to those of Italy and Germany. Although few evangelical leaders dared compare Franklin Delano Roosevelt to the Antichrist, many viewed the bureaucratic machinery erected under the National Recovery Administration as a forerunner of the future. As one spokesman said, the Roosevelt administration's intervention in economic affairs was preparation for the man prophesied in the Bible, "the big dictator, the superman, the lawless one."

Perhaps the best way to illustrate the effects of dispensationalism on evangelical political views is to recall one of born-again Protestantism's regional leaders. Gerald Burton Winrod (1900–1957) came up through the ranks of revivalism and the anti-evolution crusade to enter the field of American politics, all the while drawing upon the Bible for guidance. Winrod was a religious publisher and antagonist during the church controversies of the 1920s. His interest in and writings about politics eventually led him in 1938 to run for the Republican nomination as senator from Kansas. He first gained notoriety in 1925 with the founding of the Defenders of the Christian Faith, an organization opposed to theological modernism and evolution. Winrod wrote for and edited the Defender's publication, appropriately titled *The Defender Magazine*, while also furthering the cause as an itinerant preacher and faith healer. His work came to the attention of William Bell Riley, the head of the World Christian Fundamentals Association, who made Winrod extension secretary for the Riley organization.

Winrod's initial political instincts during the 1920s were standard fare for most evangelicals. He was opposed to evolution, gambling, strong drink, dancing, smoking, and movies, and did not mind if government intervened, as it had in Prohibition, to curtail such immorality. His indictment of Hollywood was in keeping with his more general understanding of the relationship between behavior and the soul—namely, that participation in a certain practice inevitably fractured a person's moral compass. Of filmmakers he wrote, they lured "several hundred thousand upturned faces to gaze daily at a screen which smells of filth, lust, vice, crime, and sex."

After the stock market crash in 1929, Winrod turned in a more concerted fashion to government and politics. Along with fellow religious travelers, he had followed with great interest developments in Italy and the Soviet Union, thanks to the apparent importance of those nations to biblical prophecy. But with the U.S. economic decline and the election of FDR, Winrod became so interested in Washington politics that he founded a new magazine, the *Revealer*, to alert Midwesterners to the dangers of New Deal policies. He charged that the Roosevelt administration represented a secret and systematic effort to expand the powers of the federal government in ways that resembled communism. If government intervention in economic affairs was all that Winrod needed to prove a left-ward drift in Washington, the New Deal provided lots of evidence as it generated policies and offices designed to put the United States back in the black. But Winrod's sensitivity to the slightest signs of governmental control also prevented him from seeing other problems, both in national and foreign affairs. Ultimately America's economic crisis, according to Winrod, was spiritual, and its solution required a return to true religion. This conviction led him in 1938 to enter the Republican primary in Kansas for a seat in the United States Senate, in which he finished a distant third. The excesses of his conflation of religion and politics could take him only so far.

Winrod's career points to the dark side of evangelical politics during the first half of the twentieth century. Even though he denied ever having joined the Ku Klux Klan, Winrod had supported candidates who courted Klan members and espoused the organization's white supremacist ideology. His reduction of economics and politics to religious categories also made him susceptible—as were many other evangelicals—to conspiracy theories, especially ones that centered on Jewish interests and degenerated into anti-Semitism. Of course, dispensationalism helps account for evangelical interest in Jewish life, because the prospect of Israel's reestablishment as an independent nation was key to the fulfillment of biblical prophecy.

But evangelicals' hopes for a Jewish state could also turn sinister. Winrod, for example, fell for the theory that an international Zionist conspiracy was at work, promoting both socialism and international capitalism, in an effort to undermine the United States. These views became widely held in the United States during the 1920s thanks to a series of newspaper articles by the automaker Henry Ford, later collected in a four-volume book, *The International Jew*. Ford based his reports on *The Protocols of the Elders of Zion*, a Russian fabrication that purported to be the primary documents of an international Jewish cabal. Winrod, along with the editors of such popular evangelical periodicals as *Revelation, Sunday School Times*, and *Moody Monthly*, became particularly enamored with the *Protocols* because they seemed to match the Bible's prediction about the last days. In Winrod's specific case, his belief in an international conspiracy that was following a divine plan, combined with his hostility to communism, inclined him favorably toward Hitler's opposition to communism and the German dictator's blaming of the Jews for the West's economic crisis.

Winrod was not alone in casting a sympathetic eye toward Hitler. William Bell Riley also credited Hitler with snatching the German nation "from the very jaws of atheistic Communism." An aversion to communism helps explain why evangelicals like Winrod and Riley overlooked Hitler's persecution of the Jews, since many evangelicals associated socialism and communism with Jews. But insensitivity to the plight of the Jews also stemmed from a strain of anti-Semitism, certainly shared by other Americans but particularly awkward among a group of Protestants who sought the conversion of Jews and considered themselves to be pro-Zionist. In the 1930s some evangelical leaders eventually repudiated the *Protocols* once they became convinced it was a hoax, and in turn they condemned Hitler's policies. Others, like Winrod, were not so easily dissuaded from the threat of a Jewish Communist conspiracy. Riley continued throughout the 1930s to speak of an international Jewish cabal while insisting he was not an anti-Semite. Once the United States entered World War II, he wrote *Hitlerism: or, The Philosophy of Evolution in Action*, in which he identified Hitler as the world dictator prophesied in the Bible. But Winrod's reputation as a Nazi sympathizer was not easily repudiated. His views on Germany had led him to oppose America's preparation to enter World War II. His barrage of criticism against the Roosevelt administration, both on the economy and war, eventually led to his indictment by federal officials for causing insubordination in the armed forces. After his trial and the conclusion of World War II, Winrod returned to Kansas where he continued to promote his views, though in a subdued fashion, until his death in 1957.

Although Winrod's conspiracy theories and endless speculation about spiritual forces in world history demonstrated the depths to which dispensationalism could take evangelical reflection on politics, it is also important to see that underneath these views was a middle-class work ethic. For instance, in addition to being an evangelist and would-be politician, Winrod was finally a small businessman whose outlook on the world was informed by the rigors of keeping a magazine in business. Much of his opposition to the New Deal was similar—minus the dispensationalist outer garments—to that of other small businessmen who resented government officials and banking interests setting the agenda for their welfare. According to Winrod, "Any man who will live a good life, work hard, develop his mental faculties and take advantage of his opportunities for self-advancement, can climb to the topmost rung of human achievement, under the American system of government." He spoke for most born-again Protestants in his understanding of this recipe for success in America. It was, after all, the same work ethic that Protestants had been promoting since the political and economic debates that had led to the founding of the Republican party. No matter that capitalism had become much more complicated thanks to the influence of corporations and the rise of global economies. Evangelicals remained committed to the ideals of thrift, industry, personal responsibility, and efficiency as the best guidelines for personal work habits, successful business, and a prosperous society.

In the end, business and work may have been as important for evangelical politics as were religious beliefs, no matter how powerful the teachings of dispensationalism were. Evangelicalism has been primarily a form of religious belief that emphasizes individual initiative and rewards human achievement. Entrance into the Christian faith, according to evangelicalism, depends upon the convert's free decision, not upon having been born and reared in the faith of one's parents. What is more, conversion leads to a highly disciplined and moral life where born-again believers stand more or less on their own two feet, without depending on others for help. This outlook may not automatically commit an evangelical to the principles of free enterprise and unregulated markets; but it certainly gives plausibility to the kinds of political arrangements that have benefited middle-class entrepreneurs who own or work in a family business. In fact the engine of evangelicalism, the revival meeting, bears all the marks of small-business principles applied to religion, with its carefully orchestrated advertising and publicity campaigns, its use of media, and its efficient use of workers both during and after a crusade. As Billy Graham himself once said, "I'm selling the greatest product in the world, why shouldn't it be promoted as well as soap?" Of course the entrepreneurial side of evangelicalism did not mean that born-again Protestants automatically voted the same way in national or local politics. Before the 1960s, Southern and ethnic evangelicals still tended to vote Democratic because of regional and cultural factors. Nevertheless evangelical Protestants clearly identified with the economic middle, somewhere between the wealthiest and poorest Americans, believing that the only acceptable way of life involved hard work and self-sufficiency, traits that neither the rich nor those in poverty were known to exhibit. This work ethic, fueled directly by evangelical piety, contributed greatly to the way born-again Protestants viewed domestic affairs, with dispensationalism influencing perceptions of international developments.

This fundamentally small-business outlook was evident even among evangelicals who tried to soften criticism of the New Deal and chart a new way for Christian involvement in American politics. In an important book published in 1947 that called upon evangelicals to show greater flexibility in their approach to society and politics, Carl Henry, a professor at the newly formed Fuller Theological Seminary in Pasadena, California, still found it difficult to abandon the economic assumptions that had historically informed evangelicalism. Perhaps this difficulty explained the book's title, *The Uneasy Conscience of Modern Fundamentalism*, which indicated that Henry's argument was going against the grain. In good evangelical fashion, Henry appealed to the Bible. For instance, the prophets of the Old Testament had "lashed out with uncompromised vigor against social evils of the day." The prophetic stance was a posture that evangelicals had abandoned, according to Henry, and yet if they were going to be doers and not just hearers of the Bible they would need to promote social reform. He saw a similar dynamic at work in the New Testament where, contrary to "humanist" critics who accused Christianity of endorsing the status quo, Scripture provided explicit warnings against "plundering innocent civilians" in economic matters. Of course the Bible, Henry warned, never divorced social reform from personal salvation. Like Winrod, Henry believed that the United States' and the West's political and economic problems could be solved only by the message of the gospel. But evangelicals needed to do better or else they would be an embarrassment.

Nevertheless Henry's call for a more sophisticated evangelical approach to politics ended up sounding the same themes of a middle-class work ethic. As much as he wanted evangelical churches and institutions to show greater concern for poverty and economic injustice, Henry backed away from any position that smacked of a government-assisted redistribution of wealth. So ingrained was evangelical opposition to governmental regulation of business and the collectivism of labor unions that Henry's book sounded only a faint cry against evangelical politics as usual. In one particularly revealing passage, Henry tried to forge a middle way but could not help tilting to the right:

> Is there political unrest? Seek first, not a Republican victory, or a labor victory, but the kingdom of God and His Righteousness. Then there will be added—not necessarily a Republican or labor victory, but—political rest. Is there economic unrest? Seek first, not an increase of labor wages coupled with shorter hours, with its probable dog-eat-dog resultant of increased commodity cost, but the divine righteousness: this latter norm will involve fairness for both labor and management.

Especially revealing, aside from this simple appeal to the biblical concepts of rest and righteousness as models for American society, is Henry's attempt to balance the interests of both Republicans and labor in the first question, which he loses in the second by noting the unwholesome consequences of meeting the demands of labor. The only specific policy that Henry mentions is the one advocated by the left, which ends up being opposed to "divine righteousness."

The point is not to show the clumsiness of Henry's outlook. The significance of Henry's book is that his perspective was basically that of the middle to lower middle class. This attitude informed evangelical politics even when some, like Henry, were trying to shepherd the movement away from the more extreme views of Winrod and toward a balanced biblical position. In turn, the durability of evangelical economic interests demonstrates that despite the excesses of dispensationalist theology and the speculation it generated about world leaders and the clash of civilizations, born-again Protestants were not that different from the rest of middle America. Evangelicals may not have voted with their pocketbooks, but they possessed a sense of fairness based on the simple principle that people should take responsibility for their own affairs through hard work and thrift. This was not necessarily a Republican or Democratic issue; for evangelicals it was nothing less than what the Bible required.

Dispensationalism aside, evangelicalism was not as strange a religious movement as some of its critics believed. Dispensational theology was, to be sure, the theological center of evangelical institutional life. It made itself evident in how born-again Protestants interpreted international affairs. Even so, as much as evangelicals perceived themselves as cultural outsiders and established a subculture to nurture that perception, their attitudes toward government, economics, and society were generally in the mainstream. Even as they separated themselves from the liberal mainline denominations, evangelicals continued to rely upon convictions about the religious character of the United States and the importance of Protestantism to America's prosperity that guided most Protestants, whether mainline or evangelical. This outlook favored small government, free markets, individual initiative and responsibility, and public life informed by Christian values. It viewed the United States as a Christian nation with unique responsibilities because of its religious status. With the exception of America's religious character, evangelical ideas about the behavior of individuals and governments were shared by many nonevangelical Americans who were conservative in their politics. Even the specific moral imperatives that evangelicals held to be profitable for the United States, such as abstinence from alcohol and premarital sex, were common in a society where Protestantism was still the dominant religion.

Remembering that evangelical political attitudes were chiefly ordinary is important when trying to account for a religious movement that was self-consciously marginal for at least the first half of the twentieth century and then became noticeably prominent in public life during the latter decades of the twentieth century. If evangelicals were to make a mark upon the United States, their most common interest with other Americans was not the way they interpreted the Bible or the religious entertainment they enjoyed but their politics. Billy Graham proved as much during the early 1950s. Aside from his own rhetorical skills, good looks, and accompanying musicians, he gained a national audience beyond the evangelical rank and file through the political themes of his message. As Graham's success indicated, evangelicals shared with other Americans bedrock convictions about the way societies should be ordered.

The irony is that the potential for evangelical success rested more on the earthly and temporal affairs of politics and economics than on the heavenly and eternal realities of the life to come. The subsequent rise to prominence of evangelicals in politics, foreshadowed by developments in the 1940s and 1950s, could well be construed as a betrayal of the evangelistic zeal that is supposed to characterize a movement dedicated to saving souls from everlasting judgment. But the apparent inconsistency can also be explained by the nature of evangelical religion. It insists that faith, if it is truly genuine, produces immediate results in the lives of citizens and nations. For that reason, evangelicals would not be content in their own separate subculture but would inevitably try to extend their influence into national life.

PART TWO

Preserving a Christian Society, 1960–2000

4

The Renewal of the Evangelical Mind

WHEN Fuller Theological Seminary was founded in 1947, two years before Billy Graham began showing up in the national headlines, the conventional expectations for a theological school included the training of pastors, evangelists, and missionaries, not the construction of a religious think tank that would challenge the leading assumptions of secular society in the United States and Europe. Yet at Fuller's opening exercises, students, faculty, and well-wishers heard more about the wretched state of Western civilization and the need for Christian thinking than they did about the condition of American churches and the importance of well-trained pastors.

Fuller's founding president, Harold John Ockenga (1905–1985), was the main speaker at the seminary's opening. A graduate of Westminster Seminary who had served briefly in Presbyterian congregations, Ockenga came to prominence in 1936 when he took a call to Park Street Congregational Church, a historic evangelical pulpit in downtown Boston. A Ph.D. in philosophy from the University of Pittsburgh added to Ockenga's appeal at Park Street, since part of the task confronting evangelicals in New England was to gain credibility with the region's academics. Ockenga would continue to pastor in Boston while presiding over the new California seminary, a combination that would require lots of work and travel. Perhaps in anticipation of his new responsibilities, just before Fuller's opening Ockenga had conducted a tour of Europe. He returned to the United States with a profound commitment to reconstructing Christian civilization in the West, meaning not simply California but the liberal democracies in Europe and North America. For Ockenga, Western civilization was synonymous with Christianity, as he explained in his convocation address: "You are all aware of the concept of the infinite value of individual man, which concept is being battered about in these days by men who do not believe in its source nor believe in the principles which underlie it." This fundamental concept of the dignity of the individual, upon which rested the edifice of Western politics, economics, and culture, Ockenga emphatically asserted, "is born out of the Hebrew-Christian tradition." Equally important to Western civilization was the notion of "responsibility to God." It provided the foundation for the "moral fiber of our Christian thinking, the moral fiber of the masses of the people in which they have been responsible to god and divine law."

The crisis of Western society, from Ockenga's perspective, gave the seminary under his leadership a responsibility larger than the ordinary one of training pastors, evangelists, and missionaries. Fuller needed to be not simply a school of ministerial education but also a place to contemplate evangelical theology, because this doctrinal outlook lay at the heart of the civilization that the Allies had just fought to preserve. Just as William Jennings Bryan had pointed to Germany after World War I as an example of what happened to societies that abandoned Christianity for secularism, so Ockenga was convinced that without the cardinal doctrines of Christianity a fate similar to Nazi Germany's awaited the United States and the West. "Here comes the message to America," Ockenga warned, "which is experiencing today that inner rupture of its character and culture, that inner division with vast multitudes of our people following that secularist, rationalist lie of 'scientific naturalism' in the repudiation of God and God's law." The task of Fuller Seminary, then, was much greater than providing well-educated and gifted ministers for evangelical congregations. It also involved the cultural mandate of saving Western civilization.

Ockenga's founding vision for Fuller Seminary would become the model for American evangelical intellectual life in the second half of the twentieth century. Like their predecessors, evangelicals continued to be committed to the notion that the United States bore a special role in human history and that this unique responsibility depended on the spiritual health of the nation. But unlike the generation of evangelicals who established a separate culture in order to save a faithful remnant until Christ's return, a new generation of evangelicals was emerging in the 1940s. Many of them lived and worked in the North and so were more alert than Southern evangelicals to secularization and the dissipation of Christianity's influence upon the United States. They established a new strategy of providing Christian leadership within American society. Ockenga not only represented a group of evangelicals who were better educated—many of them had Ph.D.'s from Ivy League universities—but who were convinced that the key to winning the United States back to Christ was through the contest of ideas. This was the trickle-down theory of intellectual life where right thinking inevitably produced right living. Such a theory provided born-again Protestant academics with a sense of significance and challenged evangelicals to overcome their recently acquired reputation as anti-intellectual.

Fuller Seminary was not the only school where evangelicals began thinking about the importance of intellectual life and academics for Christian witness. During the 1940s and 1950s evangelical scholars initiated a number of academic organizations whose purpose was twofold. One aim was to provide an outlet for scholars in a particular field of study to discuss and evaluate work in progress. The other purpose was to furnish evangelical scholars with the spiritual fellowship that the mainstream academic associations did not offer. In effect these scholarly organizations demonstrated the tension that evangelicals encountered once they left the religious subculture and took up residence in explicitly secular and therefore hostile surroundings. Evangelical scholars had moved beyond the amateurism of the Bible college and were learning the ropes of the secular university. At the same time they felt like strangers in a strange world. Evangelical academic societies were designed to give them solace.

The first evangelical academic organization of note was the American Scientific Affiliation (ASA), founded in 1941. Natural science was an odd sphere in which to initiate the evangelical life of the mind, since born-again Protestants had a reputation for hostility to the findings of scientists going back to the Scopes Trial. Even so, evangelicals also had an appreciation for science that went back to the eighteenth century, when Protestant theologians used the study of nature to prove the existence of God. In fact the initial impetus for the ASA came from evangelists and pastors, not professional scientists. In 1941 Will H. Houghton (1887–1947), then president of the Moody Bible Institute, wrote F. Alton Everest (1909–), a professor of engineering at Oregon State University, about the prospects of starting an organization that would demonstrate the harmony of Christianity and science. Ironically Houghton had attended only one semester of college, but that did not prevent him from emerging as one of the premier radio revivalists of the 1940s. Still, he recognized, perhaps in his capacity as president of Moody, that science was a challenge to evangelical religion. Specifically, the theory of evolution was preventing people from seeing that Christianity not only had the facts of the Bible but also the facts of nature on its side.

Even though the ASA began as an evangelistic tool, the in-

volvement of professional scientists such as Everest meant that
the organization would soon have to include a more rigorous
academic component if evangelical scholars were to continue
their membership. And Everest, who served as president
throughout the ASA's first decade, was crucial to that scholarly presence. Trained as an electrical engineer at Oregon
State College and Stanford University, Everest's specialty was
radio and television. Even though he did not earn a living
studying biology, Everest did have enough of an academic
sense to prevent the domination of the ASA by revivalists and
pastors who wanted the organization to take a firm stand
against evolution. With Everest at the helm, other evangelical
scientists emerged to give the ASA a truly academic orientation even while it remained restricted to evangelicals and
committed to the harmonization of Christianity and science,
something that most reputable scientists had abandoned fifty
years earlier.

One of those scientists who kept the ASA from going down
the path of revivalism was J. Laurence Kulp (1921–), who
used the organization as a forum for debating the simplistic
scientific claims of evangelical anti-evolutionists. Like so
many of the early leaders within the ASA, Kulp had attended
Wheaton College (Illinois) and found the school remarkably
progressive compared to the fundamentalist circles in which
he had been reared. From Wheaton Kulp went on to Princeton University for a Ph.D. in physical chemistry, and during
his time there became interested in geology, a field he pursued
with further study at Columbia University. A scholar such as
Kulp did much to steer the ASA in scholarly directions, even
while his views raised alarms about the organization within
the evangelical community.

At several of the ASA's earliest annual meetings Kulp took
on directly the most popular evangelical views about creation,
namely, that the earth was only six thousand years old and

that the Genesis account made death impossible before the fall of humankind (a view implied by the Bible's warning to Adam and Eve that if they disobeyed God they would die). The evidence of geology, Kulp insisted, pointed to a much older earth, and the fossil record indicated that death was clearly a fact of created existence well before men and women began sinning. Arguments that dismissed these geological findings as evidence of unbelieving science, and efforts to create an alternative Christian geology, one based on the flood that produced Noah's Ark, were in Kulp's words "pseudoscience." In one paper delivered at an ASA conference, Kulp claimed that "the unscientific theory of flood geology has done and will do considerable harm to the strong propagation of the gospel among educated people." Ironically, thanks to Kulp's concern for what intellectual backwardness would do to the cause of evangelism, the ASA was emerging as an organization that would do more than simply dabble in science for purposes of scoring points against the scientific establishment or proving the truth of the Bible as the ultimate book of science.

Another evangelical scholar who attempted to beef up the ASA's scientific credentials was Russell L. Mixter (1906–). A literature major at Wheaton College during the 1920s, Mixter went on for study in zoology at Michigan State University and completed a Ph.D. in anatomy at the University of Illinois School of Medicine in Chicago while teaching at his alma mater in the nearby suburbs. He tried to carve out a position called progressive creation, which interpreted parts of the first chapters of Genesis figuratively. Over time Mixter would argue for greater acceptance of evolution among evangelical scientists. To those who believed that evangelicalism was incompatible with evolution, Mixter explained that the "development of present-day forms by differentiation of previously existing forms" was "the most likely way God accomplished much of His Creation." Just as important as the details of his own views was Mixter's effort to make the ASA an organization that was committed not to defending theological propositions but to ongoing scientific inquiry.

The evangelical intellectual awakening heralded by scientists within the ASA was nonetheless fraught with difficulties. The push for tolerance of evolution led to a rift in the organization. Many rank-and-file evangelicals, especially those who viewed science as a servant of evangelism and apologetics, and who had originally pushed for an evangelical presence in scientific investigation, were unwilling to go where born-again scholars were taking them. In addition, some of those who advocated acceptance of evolution, such as Kulp, eventually tired of the battle and withdrew from various evangelical circles, proof to many opponents of evolution that secular science inevitably weakened one's faith. A further problem was the intellectual one of figuring out a sufficient rationale for an evangelical scientific organization that was committed to pursuing mainstream scholarship. The American academy offered plenty of outlets for scientists in the various fields of study. If evangelical scientists wanted professional involvement, they could easily find an academic organization that was more advanced than the ASA. In other words, the professionalization of the ASA raised the question of why evangelicals needed their own scholarly organizations. Thus the new organization was caught between the evangelical rank-and-file and the university world, a position that satisfied neither the evangelists who hoped to use science to save souls or the scientific experts who did not understand what faith had to do with reason.

But this tension between evangelistic aims and scholarly pursuits did not prevent evangelicals from forming other academic associations. Another example of evangelicalism's rising intellectual aspirations was the founding of the Confer-

ence on Faith and History (CFH), an organization of evangelical historians officially begun in 1967 but talked about as
early as the late 1950s. The origins of the CFH go back to the
1959 convention of the The American Historical Association
(AHA), the professional academic organization for historians
in the United States. At this meeting a Wheaton College professor, Earle Cairns, organized a breakfast for fellow evangelicals at the AHA. What drew them together was in part a sense
of inferiority. Many evangelicals who were interested in pursuing academic history wondered whether it was possible to
be a committed Christian and also produce distinguished
scholarship. But the historians who attended this meeting
went away with a renewed sense of calling and began to col-
lect the names of other evangelical historians who taught at
both Christian colleges and secular universities. Eight years
later the informal networks developed in 1959 paid dividends
when the CFH held its first convention at Greeneville College
(Illinois) on the "Historical Heritage of American Protestantism." Approximately seventy historians attended, in large
part because of a desire for greater cooperation and communication between those of similar faith in the same profession.
The CFH's formal statement of purpose reflected that desire
for religious camaraderie and academic pursuit. The organization's threefold purpose was to encourage evangelical scholars "to explore the relationship of their faith to historical
studies," provide a scholarly forum for a Christian understanding of history and historical methods, and "establish
more effective means of interaction" among believing historians.

Like the ASA, the CFH experienced the tension so often
felt among evangelicals: how to combine religious commitment with serious study. Just as the ASA had to ward off the
involvement of evangelicals who wanted to use science for
evangelistic purposes, so the early leaders of the CFH had to

negotiate the interests of theologians and pastors who regarded the new organization as simply another forum for intellectually interested evangelicals. The problem stemmed from the Conference's stated purpose of encouraging fellowship among evangelical historians. As one author put it in the CFH's new journal, *Fides et Historia*, "Formerly one felt strangely alone and slightly illicit in confessing both to serious pretensions as a historian and to faith in Jesus Christ as the person who died and rose again, setting one free from one's sins." But the creation of CFH was a sign that an "increasing number" of historians "found the two conjoinable." This religious side of the Conference meant that the organization was not trying to compete with the academic networks of secular historians. At the outset it sounded as if religion mattered more in joining the CFH than did scholarship. But this way of describing the Conference also opened its ranks to people who were not engaged in historical studies but who simply wanted to become acquainted with other evangelical scholars. The CFH soon confronted the problem of balancing its religious and academic missions.

Perhaps because it did not have the lightning rod of evolution, as in the case of the ASA, the CFH proved to be more congenial to nonhistorians. The early membership lists, editorial board memberships, and contributors to the Conference's journal and newsletter indicate that the organization was composed of established older historians, younger scholars fresh out of graduate school, and "history-conscious ministers and history-oriented social scientists." Noticeably present from the beginning were such evangelical theologians as Carl Henry and Harold Lindsell, who were members of the faculty at Fuller Seminary and editors of *Christianity Today*. The presence and participation of these men suggests that the CFH was better at cultivating fellowship among evangelical scholars, including historians, than it was in nurturing a decidedly evangelical approach to the teaching and study of history. Its members did not complain, largely because they had originally wanted the organization to function as a campus fellowship group for evangelical historians and their theological friends. But for those evangelicals who hoped to use the organization to engage in serious historical scholarship, as opposed to history mixed with theological reflections, the CFH was not the most congenial outlet.

This began to change as the Conference matured. A significant factor in the organization's maturation was an emphasis on professional standards, which also involved less attention to the need for religious fraternity. Over time the number of articles and papers on theological topics declined as the proficiency of historical scholarship improved. For some this represented an unfortunate departure from the organization's original purpose and the sense of camaraderie that had informed its first gatherings. But it was also a natural development for a scholarly organization dedicated to first-rate historical work. In the end, decisions about what papers to publish in a scholarly journal depended more on the quality of scholarship than on religious convictions. Thus the CFH, like the ASA, demonstrated that evangelicals were becoming more comfortable with a world that their parents and grandparents had dismissed as godless. But it also revealed that evangelical scholars were still not comfortable with the secular world and needed organizations like the CFH to give religious justification for work deemed secular. In other words, evangelical scholars, if these historians were any indication, were unsure about how the worlds of learning and faith related. A method of history based on evangelical beliefs or a school of evangelical historiography failed to emerge from this scholarly organization, in part because the demands of professional academic history left little room for explicit references to faith. Yet these evangelical historians believed that the relationship between religion and scholarship needed to be explicit if they were to retain the integrity of their religious convictions.

The one evangelical academic organization that seemed to have some *prima facie* warrant was the Evangelical Theological Society (ETS), founded in 1949 as a professional society devoted to conservative study of the Bible. The new association was originally the theological arm of the National Association of Evangelicals (NAE). It also showed the heavy involvement of professors at Fuller Theological Seminary. From the NAE's founding in 1942, it had sponsored a number of meetings for the theologians and biblical scholars in its membership. Over time these gatherings produced a call from the faculty at Gordon Divinity School, a theological seminary in Boston, Massachusetts, for a formal gathering of evangelicals who studied and taught the Bible. The initial meeting took place in Cincinnati in late December 1949 and attracted approximately sixty participants. The keynote speaker was Carl Henry, professor at Fuller Seminary.

ETS made more sense as a separate academic organization for evangelicals than, say, the ASA or the CFH because by 1950 the professional study of the Bible and theology in the United States was dominated by the mainline Protestant seminaries and divinity schools. In other academic disciplines, religion was supposed to make no difference. But in religious studies the theological convictions that had led to church controversies in the 1920s were still very much an issue, no matter how much the faculty at colleges and universities who taught religion tried to do their work dispassionately. Consequently the division between conservatives (fundamentalists) and liberals (modernists) was still at play by the time of the ETS's founding. ETS's requirement that its members affirm that "The Bible alone and the Bible in its entirety, is the word of God written, and therefore inerrant in the autographs" would have met with great opposition if not derision in such mainstream academic organizations as the National Association of Biblical Instructors or the Society of Biblical Literature, both of which were dominated by mainstream Protestants. If evangelicals were to study the Bible from the perspective that it was literally true and authoritative, they would have to cultivate their own academic organization.

ETS took a while to develop into an association with regular membership dues, its own journal, and annual and regional meetings. It was not until 1958, almost ten years after its founding, that the organization issued its first official publication, the *Bulletin of the Evangelical Theological Society*, with lists of officers and members, announcements of upcoming meetings, and the publication of selected papers. The initial issues of the *Bulletin* reveal a broad range of interests, with theology receiving more attention than biblical scholarship. They also show that in the same way the ASA offered an outlet for evangelicals who were no longer convinced of the need to oppose Darwinism, ETS provided a forum for evangelical biblical scholars and theologians to move beyond dispensationalism. Some ETS members hoped to use the authority of the Bible to uproot the theological quirks of fundamentalism. Many of the early leaders of ETS had either abandoned or held different interpretations of biblical teaching about the return of Christ. But as much as ETS may have offered a grab bag of topics for its members, one theme emerged as the organization's reason for existence—the doctrine of biblical inerrancy. This became evident at the organization's twenty-fifth anniversary when it devoted the entire contents of its journal to the subject of inerrancy, a doctrine that in its simplest terms attempted to preserve the authority and reliability of the Bible without having to figure a way to accept some parts as true and some as myth. As Millard J. Erickson admitted in his essay, while the founders of ETS had not intended inerrancy to be "the sole doctrine discussed in its circles," it had "come in for more attention than any other single area of theology during the last twenty-five years." Millard went on to argue that this was appropriate since the Bible was under considerable attack during the same period.

As much as ETS provided evangelical scholars with a view of the Bible less dependent on the categories of biblical prophecy and the end of the world, the organization's stress on inerrancy prevented these same academics from moving more freely in professional scholarly circles. The limits of this doctrine became apparent in the wake of the publication of Robert Gundry's commentary on the Gospel of Matthew, released in 1981. A professor of Bible at Westmont College in southern California who had been involved in ETS since its early days and who had often affirmed his belief in inerrancy, Gundry set off a firestorm in the ETS with his book. He argued that the apostle Matthew had introduced nonhistorical material about Jesus into his gospel in order to convey a certain theological point about the significance of Christ to his first-century audience. This did not mean that Matthew had made up events, according to Gundry, because first-century Jews would have understood the literary genre that the author was using. In that sense the Gospel of Matthew was still inerrant because its author had not intentionally sought to deceive but rather to adapt history for a larger religious purpose which ultimately was true. Since Gundry's argument depended upon specific lines of interpretation developed by secular and liberal Protestant scholars in university biblical studies, his book was an effort to bring the worlds of evangelical and secular scholarship together.

But the reaction to Gundry's book proved just how difficult it was to harmonize evangelical views with the reigning point of view in American religious studies. It also showed that inerrancy was a doctrine that could not foster unity among

evangelical biblical scholars and theologians. Gundry continued to defend his views as consistent with ETS's brief article
of faith about the Bible. But that was not how a majority of
members saw the situation. Leaders believed that Gundry had
undermined confidence in the truthfulness of the Bible, and
they persuaded rank-and-file members of the same. At its
1983 annual meeting, ETS went on record in "rejecting any
position that states Matthew or any other biblical writer altered and embellished historical tradition or departed from
the actuality of events." The vote was 119 to 36. A subsequent
vote, by a majority of 116 to 41, requested Gundry's resigna-
tion from the organization. Clearly, Gundry's own explanation of inerrancy was not sufficient to satisfy other members.
Yet ETS's own doctrinal statement was so short—only one
sentence—that it did not elaborate the implications of the belief in inerrancy or how scholars might run afoul of it. Inerrancy and the Gundry controversy isolated evangelical
theologians and biblical scholars from other scholars in the
academy precisely when evangelicals were trying to make
greater inroads in American higher and theological education.

The difficulties faced by ETS, along with those over evolution within the ASA and the CFH's awkward mixture of
piety and scholarship, all point to the fundamental tension between evangelical Protestantism and the academic world that
born-again scholars hoped to enter. Especially if religion had
to be explicitly evident in scholarship, as evangelical devotion
normally dictated, born-again Protestants were hard pressed
to attempt academic respectability at the same time they held
to a set of beliefs regarded by most academics as anti-intellectual. Still the early tensions in these evangelical scholarly organizations can also be chalked up to the kinds of growing
pains that any religious movement encounters as it matures
and attempts to become more established. In many respects
the experience of evangelical scholars during the latter half

of the twentieth century parallels that of Roman Catholic academics in the United States who went through similar struggles as they attempted to reconcile their religious and intellectual aims. But unlike Roman Catholics who possessed a religious authority in the papacy, a system of teaching in the church's theology that offered guidance about the limits of Catholic engagement with the secular academy, and a set of older academic institutions, evangelicals had a much more limited and less intellectually rigorous set of boundaries and fewer institutional resources.

Part of the awkwardness that evangelical academics were experiencing stemmed from the sense of separateness they had inherited from the conflicts and institutions of the 1930s and 1940s. At one level, evangelicals shared a common understanding of conversion and an attachment to the Bible that nurtured a sense of camaraderie among its adherents. But on another level, these sentiments did not supply mental tools sharp enough to mark intellectual guideposts for evangelicals. They did not know exactly why they were different from their secular peers in the academy and what they had in common. Thus evangelicals began to move into the world of higher education along with the rest of America's middle class, thanks to various government and academic programs designed to make college and university education more accessible. They did so, however, with a sense that the world of higher education was a foreign world to persons of evangelical convictions, and a commitment that Christianity was not only true but also essential to the success of academic endeavor.

Evangelical scholars were only one part of a broader effort by born-again Protestants to redirect American society through ideas. Emblematic of this endeavor was the 1956 founding of an opinion journal, *Christianity Today*. Although the editors listed a great many names on the magazine's masthead and sought a wide constituency, *Christianity Today* bore all the marks of the evangelical leadership that emerged during the 1940s through such institutions as the National Association of Evangelicals, Fuller Theological Seminary, and the Billy Graham Evangelistic Association. Carl Henry, a Fuller professor, was the magazine's editor, Graham's father-in-law, L. Nelson Bell (1894–1973), was a prominent supporter, and in its news columns *Christianity Today* regularly featured the affairs of like-minded evangelicals who sought a broader coalition for wider influence.

Its lead editorial, printed on October 15, 1956, not only spelled out *Christianity Today*'s reason for existence but also what would become the standard evangelical view of the relationship between ideas and social order. "A generation has grown up," the editor warned, "unaware of the basic truths of the Christian faith taught in the Scriptures and expressed in the creeds of the historic evangelical churches." This was a rebuke of the mainline Protestant churches which had "failed to meet the moral and spiritual needs of the people." But it was also the explanation for the various crises that had shaken Western society over two decades. The editor conceded that a national revival might not address all of modern society's dilemmas. Yet "statesmen as well as theologians realize that the basic solution to the world crisis is theological." *Christianity Today* was committed to applying "biblical revelation to the contemporary social crisis by presenting the implications of the total Gospel message for every area of life." With a commitment to the interdependence of "national stability" and "enduring spiritual and moral qualities," *Christianity Today* set the agenda of evangelical leaders for the latter half of the twentieth century.

One theme that stands out in the first issues of the magazine, which also indicates how evangelicals were thinking about their place in the world, is the relationship between

Christianity and culture. Perhaps because of the momentous political struggles of the time between communism in the East and liberal democracy in the West, such an emphasis is understandable, even though the magazine was supposed to include substantial attention to theological matters. But the scope of *Christianity Today*'s cultural analysis could be simply breathtaking, such as when it discussed the Western notion of freedom, the influence of the Renaissance, or the Puritan vision of society. Such heady topics may have tempted readers to think they were subscribing not to a religious periodical run by evangelical educators but to a philosophical and literary magazine edited by New York intellectuals.

In an article on "The Fragility of Freedom in the West," for example, Carl Henry began with a sweeping assertion about the differences between Western democracies and the Soviet bloc, which identified philosophical and theological problems as the most pressing for modern society. The West, according to Henry, had recognized better than the East that the nature of true freedom depended on a basic understanding of human dignity and responsibility, as opposed to the materialistic and atheistic assumptions of Marxism that governed the Soviet leaders. Even so, the Western love of liberty was on the decline. The West lacked "a passionate popular enthusiasm for liberty." The reason owed to the West's lack of a "positive philosophy of freedom." The "fuzzy and indefinite" conception of liberty in the West had "little prospect of converting the impressionable masses permanently to its side." The reason for this ambiguity stemmed from a lingering conflict in Western society between "the biblical and Renaissance traditions." In point of fact, Henry believed that the Renaissance tradition was dominating the West. As a result, notions of human dignity and responsibility appeared to be merely the preferences of specific societies without an enduring value of their own. Henry's recommendation was for the West to recover the biblical outlook, best articulated by the Protestant Reformation, where the only "compelling basis" for talking about the "inherent rights" of humankind was "the theological fact that man is a creature bearing the image of God." Only then would the ideal of liberty have a firm foundation in the "enduring distinctions of truth and goodness."

A few months later the magazine polled its contributing editors for their assessment of the cultural scene. The article's title, "Low Tide in the West," suggested the gloomy estimate turned in by the theological educators and prominent evangelical pastors who regularly wrote for *Christianity Today*. This was a curious reaction, since the evangelistic crusades of Billy Graham were receiving considerable and favorable attention and since many observers detected a religious revival sweeping across America. Yet most of the respondents believed the revival was only skin deep, and that it stemmed much more from psychological urges than sincere faith. One theology professor wrote off the revival as what happens to people in a mood of despair. They often turned "to any kind of panacea that seems to offer a solution." Another commented that "the nationwide apathy, godlessness and materialism . . . present an alarming picture and the churches are doing little more than scratch the surface of the problem." Public life on both sides of the Atlantic indicated little acknowledgment of the West's dependence on God. The editors complained that there had been no American or British statesman calling for a national day of prayer, no corporate expression of repentance. One contributor specifically faulted the working classes in Britain for showing more interest in "football pools, television and other secular hobbies" than in the things of God.

If the situation in the West was bleak, the hope was that Western society would recover its religious foundations. For the United States this meant a return to the founding vision of the Puritans. In an article on America's cultural distinctiveness, one writer contrasted the Puritan conception of society with that of the twentieth-century United States. Modern men and women were simply creatures of their culture, divorced from God—the "real source of cultural inspiration." The Puritans, in contrast, asserted that God alone "was lord of conscience," and this gave Americans the freedom to follow the dictates of their own convictions. The desire to serve God no matter what the consequence was the root, then, of American individualism and liberty. The same truth applied to modern American society, according to the author: "We can know freedom in our culture only as a free God is posited as its base. Without this assumption America will continue to lose her cultural distinctives."

To be sure, evangelicals were not alone in believing in the efficacy of ideas. Only a decade or so before *Christianity Today* was founded, the leaders of American universities had devised a number of ways to reform undergraduate education. Many of these reforms followed the same logic that right ideas produced right conduct. In such programs as the Great Books curriculum at the University of Chicago or the General Education reforms that stressed the humanities, American educators believed that acquainting young men and women with the best and noblest ideas of Western civilization would yield virtue and a renewed commitment to liberal democracy. What separated evangelical proponents of philosophical and theological renewal from other advocates of ideas was their attitude to secularism. For most American educators, Western civilization was filled with good, true, and beautiful notions that had not only informed the development of liberty and democracy in the West but could also be trusted to restore cultural order in the United States. These ideas were clearly in dialogue with Christianity, both Protestant and Catholic. But they were also the legacy of classical Rome and Greece, and so America's intellectual heritage was a happy marriage of religious and secular thought. Not so for evangelicals, who feared that secularization was precisely what ailed America specifically and the West more generally. Secular ideas promoted the notion of human autonomy from God and resulted in relativism and cultural drift. Only liberty rooted in divine rule could be trusted. The problem was trying to sell that idea to the rest of Americans, who likely saw a contradiction in the idea that true freedom could only be realized in religious submission. But evangelicals were heirs of a political and religious tradition that had always tried to harmonize the logic of American ideals with the demands of Christian theology, no matter how unsuccessful.

While the editors of *Christianity Today* carried on the battle of ideas among seminary professors and pastors, an American missionary to Switzerland escalated the conflict in amazing fashion, considering his isolation from the United States and the established institutions of American evangelicalism. Francis Schaeffer (1912–1984) took the conflict between Christian thinking and modern secularism to a new level by making popular among evangelicals the importance of ideas to ordinary life, from the way people ordered their daily lives to the way governments conducted their affairs. For Schaeffer the priority of right thinking and its necessary connection to right living could be summarized under the notion of worldview. If America were to return to its former greatness—something in doubt during the turbulent 1960s—it would also need to return to its formerly Christian worldview. At the same time Schaeffer worried that evangelicals did not have the intellectual strength to compete in the marketplace of ideas—and his ambition was to remedy that failing.

Schaeffer was an unlikely figure to emerge as the intellectual guru for American evangelicals. Born and reared in Philadelphia in a home of recent German immigrants, he came under Presbyterian influences and attended Hampden-

Sydney College in Virginia before training for the Presbyterian ministry, first at Westminster Seminary in Philadelphia
and then at Faith Seminary nearby. For almost a decade Schaeffer ministered in Presbyterian congregations in Philadelphia
and St. Louis. In 1948 he decided to pursue a call to do
missionary work in Switzerland, where he and his wife attempted to evangelize children and also helped with evangelical interdenominational Protestant efforts to counter the
influence of theological liberalism in Europe. Schaeffer's
European surroundings, particularly the intellectual and artistic currents, left an immediate impression. Through reading
and interaction with European Christians, he perceived a profound cleavage between Christian doctrine and real life. He
believed that evangelicals might have the correct theology but
that their convictions were not making a direct difference in
their lives or on the societies in which they lived. This awareness led Schaeffer to establish a community in the Swiss Alps,
near Lausaunne, which eventually became a center for young
people from Europe and North America who were looking
for answers to some of life's most vexing questions. The community was named L'Abri (French for "the shelter"), and the
trail of pilgrims who passed through the Schaeffers' home
spread the word about his interesting brand of cultural diagnosis and philosophical defense of evangelical Christianity.
Eventually Schaeffer found larger audiences in the United
States when invited by Christian campus groups to lecture before college and university students. In 1965 he emerged as
something of a celebrity, speaking at Harvard University, the
Massachusetts Institute of Technology, and Wheaton College.
These lectures gave him even greater appeal when they went
into print as the book *The God Who Is There*, published in
1968. It was the first in a trilogy that included *Escape from
Reason* (1968), and *He Is There and He Is Not Silent* (1972).
These books not only made the funny little missionary, who

wore knickers, a goatee, and long hair, more accessible to people who could not travel to Switzerland; they also registered
the basic complaint of evangelicalism against modern thought
and culture.

Schaeffer's books showed an eagerness to interact with the
great thinkers and artists of Western culture, stretching
through the Renaissance, the Middle Ages, and back to the
philosophy of Plato and Aristotle. This awareness of philosophy, art, and science gave Schaeffer immediate appeal to college-educated evangelicals who had been accustomed to
having such ideas dismissed too readily as worldly and beside
the point of evangelism. Another part of his appeal involved
his basic argument that Christianity, through the Bible, provided the only genuine basis for profound philosophy, artistic
achievement, and scientific discovery. On the one hand, this
argument reinforced the notion that what had formerly been
regarded as "worldly" pursuits were legitimate spheres for
evangelicals. On the other hand, it offered evangelicals an immediate remedy for their self-imposed cultural isolation by
proposing that the best thought and culture the West had produced was never far removed from Christian influences. Thus
evangelicals had a rationale to insert themselves in a variety of
discussions and endeavors in which they would have appeared
as upstarts. In fact, one of the dangers of Schaeffer's influence
was that he gave license to Americans who had previously ignored philosophy and art to think that now, because of their
beliefs, they had as much a right to be taken seriously as those
who had been studying these subjects all along. Nevertheless
Schaeffer did encourage evangelicals to attend to areas of hu-
manistic study they had long neglected. Even if the contrast he
drew between the God-centered philosophy and art produced
by the Protestant Reformation and that stemming from the
autonomous human reason of the Renaissance and Enlightenment was simplistic, it was also genuinely liberating for a
younger generation of evangelicals.

Schaeffer's contribution was equally important for drawing a fairly hard and fast line between good humanism, the Christian kind, and bad humanism, that of secular culture. Although Schaeffer was the first evangelical in many decades to talk openly about the value of philosophy and art, his analysis reinforced older evangelical convictions about the futility of human achievements apart from God and the Bible. Consequently, in Schaeffer's telling of European cultural history, the West crossed a definitive chasm when it made human reason, instead of the firm absolutes of the Bible, the final basis for evaluating the true, the good, and the beautiful. Twentieth-century art and philosophy, Schaeffer contended, were filled with examples of the kind of despair and relativism that resulted from denials of God's truth. He was not original in making this point. He had learned some of this from contacts he had made with Protestants in the Netherlands who stressed the importance of worldview and its influence upon culture and society. But Schaeffer made the question of worldview popular among American evangelicals. He did so by extending the evangelical idea of the Bible as the bedrock of Christian civilization in the United States to include the notion that the Bible contained truths about philosophy, art, and science. Thus it provided the basics of a Christian worldview that, if thought through and carefully applied, would result in a Christian culture. These basics started with a personal and sovereign God who had created the world out of nothing, had revealed himself in the Bible, and whose revelation was objectively true and a rule for all of life, not just for spiritual affairs. In Schaeffer's own words, this outlook was premised on the "Lordship of Christ in the totality of life." As the Lord of all things, Christ was sovereign "in spiritual matters . . . but just as much across the whole spectrum of life, including intellectual matters and the areas of culture, law, and government."

Schaeffer's ideas had obvious implications for politics and society, and in the 1970s his popularity through writing began to make a difference in the way evangelicals spoke about public life in the United States. Schaeffer himself became an outspoken critic of *Roe v. Wade*, the Supreme Court decision that legalized abortion, and with the future surgeon general, C. Everett Koop, he wrote a book which also became a film, *Whatever Happened to the Human Race?* (1979).

But perhaps Schaeffer's single greatest contribution was his popularization of the notion among evangelicals that ideas have consequences. More specifically, Schaeffer promoted the view that a person's self-understanding was crucial to the kind of conduct in which he or she engaged. The same was true for societies. Good ideas led to virtuous outcomes; bad worldviews resulted in tyranny, despair, immorality, and the loss of meaning. Schaeffer had learned this lesson first during his initial days in seminary, when he studied with Cornelius Van Til, a professor of apologetics at Westminster Seminary, who taught that Christians and non-Christians had different presuppositions or assumptions that affected the way each group looked at the world. Van Til was picking up on ideas popular among Dutch Calvinists and first originated by Abraham Kuyper, founder of the Free University in Amsterdam and prime minister of the Netherlands. Schaeffer's exposure to this way of thinking was renewed during his early days in Switzerland when he befriended Hans Rookmaaker, a historian and art critic at the Free University, who traced the decline of Western art according to the changing fortunes of a Christian worldview.

Schaeffer's adaptation of these insights from Dutch Calvinism became widely popular in the United States thanks in part to evangelicalism's earlier fixation on the Bible and evangelism. Here was a man who could talk about Immanuel Kant and Pablo Picasso with evangelicals who were increasingly heading off to colleges and universities, as well as with evangelical college faculty, both of whom lacked the ability to relate their beliefs to their learning. In the 1960s and early 1970s, as Schaeffer talked with college students and wrote his first books, his emphasis was on modern art and philosophy's loss of meaning. He tried to support his claims with a sometimes questionable history of Western art and philosophy that demonstrated the consequences of the West's secularization and its loss of a Christian worldview. For instance, in a sweeping narrative of Western culture, also made into a film, *How Should We Then Live?* (1976), Schaeffer traced the defects of modern science and philosophy to the Enlightenment's rejection of God as a foundation for inquiry and speculation. Men and women had consequently become little more than products of natural forces or historical development, with no reference to truth that transcended circumstances or place. The net result of these developments—and this is where Schaeffer's history could become heavy-handed—was Adolf Hitler and National Socialism. Nazism represented the fulfillment of the notion that the "law of nature must take its course in the survival of the fittest." Modern art showed similar signs of relativism. Pablo Picasso's painting reflected the fragmentation of the modem world; Arnold Schoenberg's atonal music rejected the certainties (God-given) of Western composition in favor of musical chaos (man-made); and Ingmar Bergman's films portrayed a universe in which God no longer spoke to his creation. Schaeffer was not always clear about whether these expressions simply reflected or were influencing the West's secularization. But he was unambiguous that modern Western society, its art and ideas, exalted the autonomy of humankind and rejected God's sovereignty.

In his later work Schaeffer thought through the effects of secularization upon American politics and society. From 1976 on he appeared to abandon the lecture circuit at colleges and universities for the public square. As he did so, his tone grew combative and his rhetoric filled with alarm. All around him he saw authoritarian governments gaining ground, thanks to secular humanism's cultivation of pragmatism and utilitarianism as the sole test for ideas or policies. In the same way that Nazi Germany had slaughtered millions of innocent lives, legalized abortion was having a similar effect. The duty of Christians, Schaeffer believed, was to return the United States to its Reformation foundation, a base he regarded as the only adequate ground for truth and morality. Thanks to these arguments, Schaeffer became known during the presidency of Ronald Reagan as the philosophical guru to the leaders of the religious right. Some of those disaffected evangelical teens and college students of the 1960s and 1970s could not entirely understand Schaeffer's image because politics seemed beneath the analysis of ideas and art. Nevertheless, despite Schaeffer's turn away from the abstractions of painting and philosophy to the realities of courtrooms and legislatures, many evangelicals learned an important lesson from him—that the path to cultural renewal lay in the realm of thought. As he wrote at the end of *How Should We Then Live?*, "The problem is having, and then acting upon, the right world view—the world view which gives men and women the truth of what is."

Signs of Schaeffer's success can be seen in the number of evangelical leaders who adopted his strategy of cultural diagnosis. One of those evangelical spokesmen was Charles (Chuck) Colson, a special counsel to Richard Nixon who was convicted of felony for his involvement in the Watergate burglary and cover-up. Colson converted to evangelical Protestantism and founded Prison Fellowship Ministries after his time in jail. From his position at the head of Prison Fellowship, Colson emerged through regular appearances on Christian radio stations and columns in evangelical magazines as one of the leading born-again critics of secular culture in the United States. His argument, like Schaeffer's, was that America's moral decay was the direct outcome of its spiritual atrophy.

In such books as *Kingdoms in Conflict* (1987) and *Against the Night* (1989), Colson demonstrated the ability, first worked out by Schaeffer, to show the connection between worldview and culture. In the former book Colson argued that modern culture, "in its zeal to eliminate divisive influences and create a self-sufficient, 'enlightened' society," had denied the fundamental truth that men and women are essentially "spiritual beings" who need God. Colson was not so simplistic as to assert that a return to Christianity would right all wrongs. In fact he was critical of some evangelicals who claimed that faith would fix the United States. But Colson did conclude that the ills of American culture and the West more generally—moral relativism, inferior public education, weak political leaders, fragmented families—stemmed from an outlook that ignored religion and faith. So too in *Against the Night*, his argument was not a crude rendition of America, as a Christian nation, needing to return to its biblical roots. He appealed instead to the development of the moral imagination and a historical awareness to counteract secular society's dehumanizing tendencies. Nevertheless Colson placed great hope in the good that such developments would accomplish. Western society had been shaped by individuals whose moral imagination had been deeply affected by Christianity, and so the battle for civilization was really a spiritual battle for the soul of modern men and women.

Colson and Schaeffer were not alone in prompting evangelicals to think about the importance of thought, but they were prominent representatives of the born-again response to the perils of secularization. From the evangelical perspective, all areas of life were profoundly religious because God is the author of all things. Secularization, in contrast, suggests that some spheres of human existence are neutral and that religion is better left out of the equation. Part of the reason for the triumph of secularization in the United States, or the decline of religion's prominence in public affairs, owed to the diversity of religious groups in the nation. Better to keep religion wrapped up in its own sphere of church and synagogue than to risk opening a public controversy among competing religious groups. Yet, because of the evangelical insistence that religion is germane to all human endeavors, and the support provided by such writers as Schaeffer and Colson about the importance of Christianity to the development of Western political and cultural institutions, secularization functioned as evangelicalism's chief rival. Secularization obviously conflicted with the evangelical belief that faith fixes problems; if religion is not allowed to enter a specific area, say politics, then the possibility of a lasting solution is gone. The evangelical case against secularization, then, made perfect sense. But it also made evangelical arguments about religion and culture sound irrelevant if not outdated, because the United States was trying to accommodate religious diversity during the same years that figures like Colson and Schaeffer were making their strongest case. Despite the increasing sophistication of evangelicals in their intellectual efforts, born-again opposition to secularization blinded them to other aspects of cultural development, such as economic and political factors. Thus the emphasis on competing worldviews reinforced the evangelical habit of looking only at the abstract realm of the spirit instead of the concrete one of how the world works.

After the Scopes Trial, evangelical Protestantism became a topic of derision, at least in scholarly circles. In the words of R. Laurence Moore, "In America's best-known centers of learning, [evangelicals] were losing a battle of prestige." But in the second half of the twentieth century born-again Protestants attempted to overcome that loss of status in learned circles, partly because American higher education became much more accessible to all Americans and partly through hard work and ingenuity. Evangelical fortunes appeared to change sufficiently for the *Atlantic Monthy* to print a cover story in 2000 on the evangelical mind. To be sure, the author did not compare Wheaton College to Harvard University. But he did document the seriousness with which evangelicals pursued higher learning. Questions remain about the capacity of evangelicals to contribute in creative and original ways to the life of the mind on the basis of their narrowly defined faith. But for any reader familiar with evangelicalism's earlier reservations about higher education, the change signaled by this piece was remarkable.

Underneath this reversal of the verdict on the evangelical mind remained an abiding conviction about the relationship between right thinking and right behaving. Just as William Jennings Bryan had criticized Darwinism for its destructive moral and cultural consequences, so evangelical scholars and public spokesmen linked ideas that denied the truths of Christianity with moral relativism and social purposelessness. By connecting ideas to their personal and social consequences, evangelicals demonstrated their inherently pragmatic orientation, which evaluated ideas—but more than that, institutions, power, economic relations, and cultural expression—in relation to their practical outcome. This pragmatic outlook has made evangelicals effective communicators in a society that also evaluates life more by results than by theories. But it has also subjected evangelical views to the burden of being wrong about the connection drawn between certain ideas and specific consequences. Nevertheless the evangelical mind shows the characteristic mark of born-again Protestantism's urge to make religion relevant and apply it to daily life.

5

Evangelical Politics and the Religious Right

IN 1976 evangelicals moved from the cultural margins to center stage, at least in the eyes of America's major news media. That year saw Chuck Colson's book about his own conversion to evangelical Protestantism, *Born Again*, sell more than a half-million copies. And during that year's presidential contest, Jimmy Carter, the Democratic nominee and eventual winner of the November election, revealed himself to be a "born-again" Christian. Such growing prominence of born-again Protestantism led the editors of *Newsweek* magazine to declare 1976 "the year of the evangelical."

If that was so, 1980 was the year of evangelical politics. The presidential race in 1976 had featured two candidates who had played up their evangelical identity, Jimmy Carter and Gerald Ford. But the 1980 race featured a third-party candidate, John Anderson, who along with Carter and the eventual winner, Ronald Reagan, claimed to have been born again. That year was also significant because it was the first post–World War II presidential election in which evangelical voter turnout had a palpable affect on the results. In 1979 Jerry Falwell, a Baptist minister in Lynchburg, Virginia, had founded the Moral Majority, an organization dedicated to electing "moral" candidates for public office and functioning as a watchdog of

America's Christian values. Although assessments of Reagan's victory differ regarding evangelicalism's influence, there is little doubt that groups like Falwell's Moral Majority functioned as a catalyst to get out the evangelical vote. This election was pivotal not simply to the emergence of the religious right but for evangelicalism, a movement once discredited as irrelevant and culturally isolated. It was now reasserting its presence in American life.

Debates also continue about the religious character of the religious right. Some argue that organizations such as the Moral Majority did not represent genuine evangelicalism. Falwell himself claimed to be a fundamentalist, and mainstream evangelical leaders such as Billy Graham and magazines such as *Christianity Today* did not endorse the Moral Majority or its tactics. Consequently some will speak of a difference between evangelical and fundamentalist political involvement, the former being more moderate and interested in consensus, the latter being more radical and belligerent. To be sure, as born-again Protestant political activities have grown, evangelicals have revealed different ideas about the best way to cultivate a godly society. But although they may not always agree on certain policies or vote for the same candidates, and although some may be more comfortable with the fundamentalist label than others, evangelicals share a common outlook that is unmistakably the product of born-again Protestantism.

Two convictions are at the heart of evangelical politics. The first concerns the Bible as the supreme authority for faith and life, with life being construed in its widest sense. The Bible, accordingly, is the rule for politics and social organization as much as it is for worship and personal morality, because it is the only trustworthy standard. The evangelical affirmation of biblical authority rarely yields agreement on what the Bible teaches about politics or the best form of social order. It does, however, indicate that born-again Protestants are uncomfortable with human as opposed to divine standards or authorities. Consequently the most reliable guide to life, whether public or private, is one that comes directly from God; all other political philosophies or ideologies are simply the product of fallen and fallible men and women. Because the Bible is accessible to all believers, no matter their ability to interpret it, the evangelical regard for Scripture yields a populist political style. Born-again Protestants are generally suspicious of elites and privilege, an outlook that further erodes interest in systematic reflection on power and authority.

The second religious conviction that informs evangelical politics is the born-again experience. Conversion is also a great leveler of privilege and rank because it results in a sanctified person who is capable of intuiting what is just or right in social and international affairs. In other words, being born again results in holy instincts about the way societies should be ordered and governments run. And because genuine conversion is supposed to produce certain virtuous behaviors along with restraint from sinful ones, it orients evangelicals toward political issues with ethical or moral significance. When they mobilize for political endeavor, evangelicals do so most often by evaluating a policy or piece of legislation on the basis of whether it conforms to divine will. In sum, beliefs about the Bible and conversion drive evangelicals to approach politics as something where faith is at stake.

If this outlook is a constant among evangelicals, the question is why these Protestants became so engaged politically when they did. Here the explanation relies as much on changes in American society during the 1960s as on the emergence of new and successful evangelical leaders and organizations. Put simply, after 1960 the United States entered a new phase of cultural history in which Protestantism no longer yielded a common sense of purpose and set of standards as it once had. The resurgence of evangelicals in American politics since the 1960s can be explained chiefly as a reaction to this situation. Evangelicals themselves did not think that what they were doing was new. Indeed, their political involvement and instincts ran in the same grooves that had directed previous generations of evangelicals. But the change in America, from a Protestant to a post-Protestant society, made evangelical politics appear to many as old-fashioned, if not a little obnoxious.

Yet as much as changes in American life help to account for the rise of a "religious right," one important variable among evangelicals themselves that altered their public presence was the ascendency of Southern born-again Protestants. After all, Jimmy Carter, the first twentieth-century president to speak openly of being born again, was a devout Southern Baptist from Georgia. The man who founded the Moral Majority, Jerry Falwell, was a Baptist minister from Virginia. Of course, the South contributed more to American life than simply those evangelicals who engineered the religious right, as the industrial and commercial growth in such Sun Belt cities as Atlanta, Charlotte, Orlando, and Houston suggests. But the rise of Southerners as spokesmen for the evangelical movement was significant in part because the culture of the South provided a better base for political action than the North. Unlike Northern evangelicals, who developed a plan for gaining intellectual clout by taking on the philosophical foundations of secular culture, Southern evangelicals wanted to preserve a culture in which born-again religion was dominant. Whereas Northerners had already come to terms with their marginal status, evangelicals from the South were less squeamish about asserting the importance of religion in the public square because Southern society had been so clearly shaped by born-again Protantism. Both groups shared a common outlook, but Southern evangelicals had more to lose if the South followed the same cultural and political path as the North.

An important book appeared in 1972 that both reflected evangelicalism's heightened political awareness and defined the terms on which born-again Protestants would often evaluate their political involvement. It was David O. Moberg's *The Great Reversal: Evangelism versus Social Concern*. Then a sociologist at Milwaukee's Marquette University, Moberg diagnosed what he believed to be evangelicalism's withdrawal from politics and social reform. In the nineteenth century, he argued, evangelicals had not distinguished evangelism or the saving of lost souls from efforts to make their society more equitable and righteous. In fact, Moberg believed that the contemporary division between evangelicals who tried to save sinners and liberal Protestants who endeavored to save society offered an unfortunate choice between two extremes. What was needed was a balanced approach. Here Moberg recommended examples from evangelical history, before the so-called great reversal when the modernist-fundamentalist controversy pulled apart religious concern for the eternal destiny of the soul from a humanitarian interest in reforming society. Only by returning to an older Protestant awareness of the interdependence of body and soul could late twentieth-century evangelicals be fully "scriptural."

Moberg's book functioned as a wake-up call for many evangelical academics who were tired of the movement's identification with the Republican party. It also reinforced the argument of a book, published only two years earlier in the same series by a historian at Indiana State University, Richard V. Pierard, *The Unequal Yoke*, that complained vigorously about evangelicals as mere "handmaidens of the Far Right." Some rank-and-file evangelicals would no doubt be confused by the mixed signals in these books. On the one hand, these authors told evangelicals they were guilty of abandoning politics and social concern because of their interest in evangelism. On the other hand, they rebuked evangelicals for their infatuation with big business, anti-communism, and Republicans. So which was it? Was the problem that evangelicals had withdrawn from politics, or that their political involvement was of the wrong kind? Despite their confusing message, Moberg and Pierard had put their collective finger on an apparent problem. Evangelicals had at one time been more active in and comfortable with public life. But since the 1930s the movement had prospered as a religious subculture, and its most audible political voices were usually associated with the far right. Was it possible for evangelicals, these books asked, to supply the nation with political leadership not just for themselves but for all Americans?

One point lacking in Moberg's and Pierard's analysis was attention to a number of 1960s issues that had prompted evangelicals to leave the comfort of their religious subculture for the contentious environment of the public arena. Here it is important to note the benefits that evangelicals enjoyed in American society before 1965, thanks to the work of their theological adversaries, the mainline Protestant churches. The culture of the United States during the middle decades of the twentieth century, even in the diverse Northeast, did not overly threaten evangelical Protestants. Born-again believers had in many cases abandoned the mainline churches, and so on Sunday mornings they were not sitting in the same pews as Protestants for whom the Bible and conversion were less important. But as much as they might complain about the defections of the mainline Protestant denominations, evangelicals did benefit from the generically Christian culture that the mainstream churches had preserved. Thus evangelicals could send their children to public schools with some confidence because the school day opened with prayer and Bible reading. Public schools were also less threatening to born-again Protestants before 1965 because parents did not have to fear that their children would be bused to a faraway school in order to compensate for the way laws and suburban development had segregated whites and African Americans. Nor did evangelicals have to worry about the dangers and consequences of sexual liberation for men and women, because the churches generally condemned contraceptives, and abortion was illegal. Equally important to evangelicals on the home front was a set of mores that established child-rearing and homemaking as God-ordained responsibilities for women. And while evangelicals may have avoided the products of Hollywood, mainline Protestants displayed a similar suspicion of the movies when they advocated a ratings system based on conventional Protestant morality. In sum, America during the 1950s was closer to the kind of society that evangelicals who became more politically active after 1965 wanted; it offered standards of public decency. Evangelicals may have been on the sidelines of politics from 1930 to 1970 partly because they did not need to be in the fray.

But from an evangelical perspective, America changed decisively in the 1960s into a godless society, and this transformation also changed born-again Protestants into socially and politically involved citizens. The chief catalysts propelling evangelicals into the public arena were a series of events that threatened the way parents passed on their faith to their children. Here the so-called sexual revolution was an obvious danger for evangelicals. Not only did the encouragement of relaxed standards for sexual relations violate Christian teaching about chastity and marriage, but the more relaxed understanding of sex was also part of a new attitude toward femininity and child-bearing which directly challenged the cult of domesticity that prevailed among most born-again Protestants. Feminism compounded the problem by raising further questions about the desirability of domestic life and child-rearing as a source of fulfillment for women. When the Supreme Court ruled that abortion should be legal, evangelical concerns shifted from issues about a woman's proper role to the much more basic one of sparing the lives of innocent human beings.

If these fundamental challenges to the evangelical understanding of the family were not sufficient, changes in public schooling further eroded born-again Protestant confidence about the United States as a suitable place for rearing children. The removal of prayer and Bible reading from opening exercises in schools, thanks to a series of Supreme Court rulings, revealed to evangelicals the anti-religious bias of many politicians and educators. At the same time policies stemming from the civil rights movement, designed to achieve the racial integration of public education, forced some children to attend schools outside their neighborhood. Finally, the anti-Americanism launched by Vietnam War protesters further alienated evangelicals because of their convictions about the United States' divinely appointed role in human history. In sum, practically all the social movements of the 1960s that divided the left and the right in American politics pushed evangelicals even farther in a conservative direction. And these movements motivated evangelicals to become directly involved in the political process.

The effects of these challenges to the family and the prerogatives of parents were clearly evident in the way evangelical discussions of politics shifted from the 1960s to the 1970s. During the period before *Roe v. Wade* (1973), evangelicals continued to assess American society and the nation's involvement in international affairs primarily in the received categories: liberty over tyranny, free markets over planned economies, individual responsibility and the work ethic over welfare, and religion as the bedrock of national morality over relativism and secularism. For instance, in the pages of *Christianity Today*, which by the 1960s had emerged as the magazine of record for evangelical Protestantism, the dominant political themes were those of mainstream conservatism—liberty, capitalism, law and order, and patriotism. Thus the magazine's editors defended free enterprise against the growth of big government. The latter drew especially heated attacks when it took the form of communism, and evangelicals often claimed that only a slippery slope separated American liberals from socialists. This position also included support for America's efforts to halt the spread of communism and a variety of calls for evangelicals to display their loyalty to the United States which, despite its problems, was still the greatest nation on earth. But freedom had its limits, and the editors of *Christianity Today* could not defend a liberty that resulted in social chaos or anarchy. Consequently, at the same time evangelicals defended free markets, they denounced hippies and other radicals who challenged American institutions and values. *Christianity Today* even functioned as an outlet for FBI director J. Edgar Hoover, who wrote pieces in the magazine lamenting lawlessness and civil disobedience.

Similar themes can be found in the work of two prominent evangelical leaders, Billy Graham and Carl Henry. The former continued his popularity as the most visible evangelical and established his reputation as the greatest revivalist in American history. He worked through crusades but also through a variety of other endeavors, including radio broadcasts, magazine publishing, and even cinematography. Graham himself avoided overtly political topics in his speaking, but his concern for the nation's well-being inevitably prompted him to address social matters. In this sense he was a celebrated patriot who could be counted on to bolster support for American ideals. In 1970, for example, he participated with the comedian Bob Hope and the *Reader's Digest* in Honor America Day, and a year later he led Pasadena's Tournament of Roses Parade as grand marshal. Graham was so respected that presidents courted his friendship and support. Often he returned the favor, such as when he publicly supported the Vietnam War during the Johnson and Nixon administrations, a decision based as much on anti-communism as on personal ties to the president. Yet the evangelist could be critical of the United States. He feared that its ideal of liberty could easily be abused to encourage immorality, and he regularly denounced pornography, adultery, divorce, homosexuality, and drugs. At the same time Graham was also critical of racial segregation and gave cautious support to various efforts to improve race relations, from having an integrated staff to making television advertisements in which he urged Americans to comply with legislation that mandated the integration of public schools. But again, these criticisms were designed to help the United States live up to its religious heritage, not question its political foundations.

Carl Henry, who edited *Christianity Today* for most of the 1960s and emerged at the same time as a prolific theologian, devoted more time than Graham did to political reflection, but he continued to walk in well-worn paths. One of the themes in Henry's writing on America that distinguished him from Graham was the idea that social involvement was a duty for all Christians. In other words, evangelism was not a sufficient expression of Christian concern for others. But when it came to the precise form this activity should take, Henry was guarded and implicitly conservative. He criticized big government as much as he denounced the social gospel of the mainline churches. At the same time Henry was not so suspicious of either the state or the church's social responsibility as to ignore the positive role that government could play in maintaining peace and order, or the contribution of the church in articulating ideals of justice and righteousness. Like most evangelicals of his generation, although he worried about the spread of immorality in American society Henry was a loyal citizen who believed in the unique goodness and responsibility of the United States. Consequently the patriotism that informed his writings provided the glue for evangelicalism's social outlook during the two decades after World War II. Displaying support for and trying to make the United States a more godly society was the chief concern of mainstream evangelicalism as articulated by such leaders as Henry, Graham, and *Christianity Today*'s editors and writers.

Of course, evangelical political reflection before *Roe v. Wade* contained its share of appeals to the Bible and born-again morality. These were evangelical staples. Yet, despite these telltale signs of evangelical thought, the political aims of the neo-evangelical leadership of the 1950s and 1960s were to contribute to the health of the nation. After the 1960s, however, the orientation of evangelical political attitudes and actions changed from preserving the United States to the more narrow aim of protecting the American family. It was not absolute: concern for the family cannot be isolated from national politics since government has increasingly extended its oversight into affairs once regulated solely by families. Consequently evangelical politics in the era of the religious right includes both family values and small government, the idea being that the state needs to get out of the way and let parents oversee their own affairs. At the same time the shift toward the family in evangelical politics during the 1970s, spearheaded by the rise and prominence of the religious right, stemmed not simply from a specific commitment to limited government but also from a sense that the family was besieged by secularism and immorality, and that the United States government was too often aiding and abetting forces harmful to rearing godly and responsible children. This is why the sexual revolution, feminism, abortion, and changes in public education are crucial for understanding evangelical politics in the late twentieth century. These developments were a prelude to the rise of the religious right. They switched evangelical social concerns from domestic issues (in a national sense) to issues of domesticity.

This shift was well illustrated in an article that appeared in *Christianity Today* just after the last of the Supreme Court's rulings prohibiting prayer and Bible reading in public schools. The author, Ronald C. Doll, who taught education at New York City's Hunter College, argued that evangelicals had been caught completely off guard by the Court's decision. In his estimation, they not only secularized the schools but made it possible for children to be taught atheism or agnosticism without any opposing perspective. For this reason Doll urged evangelicals to look beyond the public schools for assistance in building "our children's faith." They needed specifically to think about ways to teach born-again Protestant children the content of Christianity outside the public school. This involved training teachers who could provide a Christian education and constructing a curriculum that would follow children through their intellectual development. Doll did not advocate forming Christian schools or home schooling—though a sidebar to his article in the magazine was a piece on "The Power of the Home," which asserted that "no child will forever get away from the influence of a Christian mother or a Christian father." Instead Doll's recommendation was an allotment of time during the public school day when evangelical children would be released for religious education. Such released-time programs had been in effect since the 1940s and had even passed Supreme Court scrutiny. Even so, Doll's article demonstrates how changes in American public policy that affected the ability of parents to teach and rear their children prompted evangelicals to circle the wagons in defense of the almighty home.

The shift toward family values was also evident in southern California, an important locale for three reasons. First, in Orange County the particular mix of evangelical and political conservatism provided the blueprint for the religious right as a national movement. Second, evangelical concerns in the suburbs of Los Angeles suggested to conservative political strategists a platform for attracting wider support for Republican candidates, even from disaffected voters in the Democratic party. Finally, California's religious conservatives proved to be important in identifying the political candidate upon whom the religious right would pin many of its hopes—Ronald Reagan, who used his office as governor of California as a beachhead for becoming the fortieth president of the United States.

Beginning in the late 1960s, in response to a series of Supreme Court decisions that granted greater freedom in sexual expression, evangelicals in Orange County mobilized to defend traditional roles for men and women and the sanctity of the home. For instance, when Supreme Court justices made pornography more difficult to prosecute, California conservatives responded with legislation that redefined pornography and gave local officials greater authority in prosecuting obscenity. Although the legislation failed in a statewide referendum, it gained Governor Reagan's strong support and further concentrated conservatives' attention on questions of public morality. Another issue that heightened evangelical and conservative fears was sex education. In 1969 Orange County conservatives successfully eliminated from local public schools a program of sex education that was a pilot project for the Sex Information and Education Council of the United States. Although the curriculum had been developed in consultation with local clergy and community groups and taught the negative consequences of premarital sex, its evangelical critics denounced it as "godless, pornographic, and an affront to family privacy." Aside from what this reaction says about evangelical mores, this incident was also critical for showing conservatives how to turn an ethical issue into a matter of politics. Here California evangelicals appealed to the notion that educators were usurping the authority of parents and turning children against the values of the home. Some parents even used the language of conspiracy to account for the waywardness of teenagers. Thanks to evangelical arguments, the program was drastically scaled back in Orange County, and California Republicans adopted a resolution that called for the abolition statewide of sex education programs.

California conservatives were not as successful when it came to abortion, the most important issue for mobilizing evangelicals politically and making family values the center of their activism. During the late 1960s California implemented a number of laws that permitted access to abortion for mothers facing threats to their physical or mental health because of pregnancy. Before these changes, abortions when performed were done so illegally. Although these new laws were still restrictive, by the early 1970s the California courts had invalidated nearly all of those restrictions. In effect, by 1972 an abortion could be obtained on demand. Orange County evangelicals were alarmed by these decisions, first because they believed abortion was killing a human life and therefore an act of murder. But aside from abortion being a violation of the Ten Commandments, it was also an activity with implications about a woman's proper role as a nurturer and caregiver. From an evangelical perspective, abortion was the logical conclusion of feminism. Although a number of evangelical women on the national scene tried to harmonize women's equality in society with biblical teaching about gender roles, the feminist movement's support for a woman's right to choose made women's liberation just one more sign of a society-wide assault upon the traditional family. California conservatives, with their national partners, could not block the legalization of abortion, but this issue gave evangelicals further incentive to enter the political arena. It provided the platform for founding political organizations and networks that would be the building blocks of the religious right. Abortion also proved to be a divisive issue for Roman Catholics, a traditional Democratic constituency, who began to form alliances with evangelical Protestants and moved in the direction of the Republican party.

What the experience of California conservatives demonstrates is how much American mores were changing in ways that evangelicals particularly found objectionable. Jerry Falwell summed up the evangelical political initiative well when he identified the "Imperative of Morality" as the foremost issue facing American society. And the frontline in the battle for the United States was the family. It was the institution that finally led him to become involved in politics. As he explained his decision to found the Moral Majority,

> The government was encroaching upon the sovereignty of both the Church and the family. The Supreme Court had legalized abortion on demand. The Equal Rights Amendment, with its vague language, threatened to do further damage to the traditional family, as did the rising sentiment toward so-called homosexual rights.

Someone finally had do to something about what Falwell called "this moral chaos." The Virginia Baptist pastor may have been the evangelical to gain the national spotlight in being that someone. But more important to the rise of the religious right was the perceived sense of "moral chaos" and its threat to the family. It created a political itch that evangelicals were bound to scratch. Ironically—as many critics of the evangelical right would point out—the moral chaos that Falwell perceived in the United States had not been evident in the South's laws enforcing racial segregation. When in the 1960s black ministers championed the cause of civil rights for Africans Americans, many Southern evangelicals insisted upon the separation of church and state, arguing that ministers should be above politics. But that argument no longer applied in the 1970s because the threat to the evangelical way of life was apparently so formidable.

The emergence of a conservative Protestant voice in American politics conjured up associations with the old Christian right of the 1930s. A number of historians and political scientists have argued that the evangelical politics of the 1970s and 1980s is simply an updated version of religiously inspired right-wing politics that have surfaced regularly in twentieth-century America. According to this view, the first stage occurred during the 1920s when fundamentalists participated actively in campaigns against alcohol, Catholicism, and evolution. After the 1920s conservative Protestants identified the New Deal as the enemy and became virulently anti-Communist, though they showed affinities for fascism and anti-Semitism. During World War II evangelical politics moved back toward the moderate middle but retained its animosity to communism and socialism. The second phase of the Christian right emerged during the 1950s, this time led by such well known anti-Communist preachers as Carl McIntire and Billy James Hargis. As long as fears of Communist conspiracies remained high, the Christian right looked somewhat respectable. In the aftermath of Senator Joseph McCarthy's abusive search for Communists in the United States and Barry Goldwater's unsuccessful campaign for president in 1964, the fortunes of political conservatism declined and the Christian right returned to its position of isolation. But with the religious right's reassertion of faith into politics through the Moral Majority and the 1980 election of Ronald Reagan, who gained the endorsement of most evangelicals, scholars believed they were witnessing the return of the Christian right to United States politics. In fact the earliest books and articles on evangelical politics during the 1980s referred to Falwell and the Moral Majority as the "New Christian Right," a phrase implying that the religious right was simply the latest rendition of the old evangelical politics of the 1930s and 1940s.

Although a commitment to conversion and the Bible unites evangelical politics across the decades, this way of looking at the religious right of the late twentieth century misses an important difference. Evangelicals involved in politics during the depression and World War II were generally interested in national and international politics and economics. They identified collectivism, both at home (the New Deal) and abroad (communism and socialism), as the chief enemy to American liberty. As evangelicals who saw most problems through a spiritual lens, they accounted for communism's errors by looking to the Soviet Union's atheism. For the religious right of the later years, however, the most pressing issues facing the United States were not necessarily economic or political but personal. This explains why evangelicals shifted from American to family values. Undoubtedly the turn toward domesticity did not involve abandoning convictions about the United States, its best form of government, or its involvement in international politics. Evangelicals continued to identify with the right and to oppose collectivism wherever they detected it, whether in the Soviet Union or the Democratic party. Still, during the 1970s the greatest threat to evangelicals was no longer communism but an enemy that denied the existence of God and even questioned the morality that made traditional family life possible.

That enemy was secular humanism. Over the last quarter of the twentieth century, this phrase energized evangelicals the way communism had between 1920 and 1970. The person who gave this notion credibility was Francis Schaeffer, the man who almost singlehandedly alerted evangelicals to the dangers and virtues of art, philosophy, and music, realms of life previously neglected by born-again Protestants. The importance of secular humanism to Schaeffer's diagnosis of Western civilization had been there from his earliest writings in the 1960s. Secular humanism's roots lay in the Renaissance and the Enlightenment, when philosophers began to assert humankind's autonomy from God and subsequently made "man the measure of all things." Until the late 1970s Schaeffer attempted to persuade evangelicals to take ideas seriously, and to persuade nonevangelicals to see the consequences of a secular worldview, one that left them without meaning and values. But in the late 1970s, just as evangelicals were beginning to become a force in electoral politics, Schaeffer applied his understanding of worldviews to American society and attempted to show how secular humanism was at the root of the United States' moral decay. In a book and companion film series, *Whatever Happened to the Human Race?*, he specifically targeted abortion as evidence of secular humanism's destructive influence. The book's co-author was C. Everett Koop, an evangelical pediatrician in Philadelphia well known for pioneering work in neonatal surgery. The book and movie were pivotal in Ronald Reagan's selection of Koop to serve as surgeon general of the United States.

Proof of Schaeffer's importance in popularizing the idea that philosophies have cultural and political consequences can be found in the work and writings of Tim LaHaye. A pastor in San Diego who first became active in politics during the southern California battles over family issues in the late 1960s, he went on to lead a number of institutions, among them Family America (1979), and write books dedicated to preserving marriage and the family. (He is also the co-author of the best-selling novel series, *Left Behind*, discussed in the next chapter. LaHaye's wife, Beverly LaHaye, was instrumental in the 1978 founding of Concerned Women for America, the conservative alternative to the feminist National Organization of Women.) What motivated LaHaye to greater social activism beyond local California politics was a sour estimate of the first president to make being born-again a badge of honor, namely, Jimmy Carter. Although he talked a good game, Carter showed greater tolerance on gay rights and feminist issues than many evangelicals could bear. LaHaye not only threw his support behind Reagan in the 1980 election but began to trumpet the idea, learned from Schaeffer, that the cause of America's corruption was ultimately intellectual. Secular humanism, then, was public enemy number one, and La-Haye, following Schaeffer's analysis, further popularized the notion that growing disregard for the family, sexual liberation, and abortion stemmed from the ideas of the Renaissance and Enlightenment.

For example, in the first of a three-volume series on values in American culture, *The Battle for the Mind* (1980), a book dedicated to Francis Schaeffer, LaHaye went directly to the source when he asserted that "Today's wave of crime and violence in our streets, promiscuity, divorce, shattered dreams . . . can be laid right at the door of secular humanism." Put simply, humanism, according to LaHaye, was "man's attempt to solve his problems independently of God." From this premise he went on to document the dominance of humanism in the United States, usually following Schaeffer's own intellectual history of modern Western thought. Humanism was responsible for atheism, rationalism, socialism, existentialism, evolution, Freudianism, and communism. It triumphed in Europe in the late eighteenth century with the terrors of the French Revolution but did not become prominent in the United States until the 1930s. This was the period when, in LaHaye's and Schaeffer's analysis, the federal government expanded exponentially and began its control of American education. Secular humanism's victory in the United States, however, was fundamentally at odds with the nation's Christian origins. In a revealing line about American history, LaHaye declared that "as long as biblical thought prevailed in the public-school system, there was no real need for pro-moral people to put on a drive to get moralists elected to government office." As this quotation suggests, evangelicals were generally content with the main features of American society until the 1960s. But everything changed once evangelical parents felt that their ability to pass on their faith to another generation was threatened by public institutions.

LaHaye's appeal to morality was another striking feature of his book. This provided the basis for his call to greater political involvement from his conservative readers. His first piece of advice was for evangelicals to pray, and he included a chart designating the federal and local officials who should be the object of their prayers. He also advised greater commitment to personal evangelism. But the bulk of LaHaye's recommendations concerned politics. He argued that conservatives should vote for and volunteer to help "pro-moral" political candidates; they should also work vigorously to oppose "amoral" candidates and incumbents. To this end he added an appendix with a checklist for determining whether a politician was moral or not. The first five questions on this guide were addressed to: (1) the United States' biblical origins; (2) abortion; (3) feminism; (4) prayer in public schools; and (5) pornography. Out of twenty-one questions, seven concerned primary and secondary education, six involved legislating morality, and five addressed scaling back the federal government. Although the tension between advocating small government and expanding the state's reach through laws regulating immoral behavior went unnoticed, LaHaye's grid of evaluation aptly illustrated evangelicalism's guiding political instincts. In addition, his plug for the fittingly named Moral Majority linked his own work and thought to the first of evangelicalism's most visible attempts to flex its political muscle.

LaHaye was not the only proponent of the Moral Majority

that Schaeffer influenced. Jerry Falwell, the founder of the organization, also proved to be fertile ground for Schaeffer's understanding of culture. So impressed was the Baptist pastor with Schaeffer's film series *How Should We Then Live?* that he made it required viewing for freshmen at Falwell's own institution, Liberty University. Under Schaeffer's direction too, Falwell recognized the importance of academic institutions in training future leaders, and he endeavored to make Liberty the Harvard University of Protestants. Even more important, however, was Schaeffer's argument that evangelicals needed to be active in politics. Proof of its persuasiveness came in 1979 when Falwell joined with several other prominent religious broadcasters to found the Moral Majority. This organization was not simply a consequence of cultural analysis or theological nuance. It was also the product of secular conservative political strategists who saw morality as an opening for the Republican party to recapture the White House. Specifically, Paul Weyrich and Richard Viguerie, who had labored in Republican circles for decades, spotted a new base of support among evangelicals. They also believed that a strong moral component in the Republican party's platform, especially opposition to abortion, might tempt Roman Catholics, a traditional Democratic constituency, to switch parties. Such a strategy appeared to be the right one when Ronald Reagan, a divorcee and non-church member who claimed to be a born-again Christian, defeated the incumbent, Jimmy Carter, decisively and carried a number of Democratic constituencies.

The usefulness of the Moral Majority to the Republican party was obvious throughout the Reagan presidency. Although it alienated many Americans, the organization's checklist for what LaHaye called "pro-moral" candidates gave the Republican party a new base of support. The Moral Majority also tapped evangelicalism's knack for spreading the word by developing a fairly large membership (in 1980 it took the lead in registering approximately four million new voters) and granting members the independence through local chapters to pursue moral issues at the grassroots level. So, for instance, the Maryland chapter of the Moral Majority attracted attention when it planned a boycott of a bakery that was selling gingerbread cookies in "sexually explicit" shapes. But aside from sponsoring patriotic rallies and focusing media attention on public morality, the teaching of evolution in the public schools, and specific candidates, the Moral Majority earned for evangelicalism much negative publicity because of its apparent ethical smugness and Falwell's own inability to play the game of public relations. By 1989 the Moral Majority had folded. In his announcement, Falwell declared the organization was no longer necessary because it had achieved its goals. Some believed, however, that the Moral Majority's leaders had been frustrated by the political process, had seen their support do little to change the moral tenor of American society, and had closed the organization's doors because they did not seem to be making a difference.

Falwell's decision to shut down the Moral Majority was made easier by the emergence of Pat Robertson, another television evangelist, and his organization, the Christian Coalition, to carry on the aims of the religious right. The son of a former United States senator from Virginia and a graduate of Yale Law School, Robertson became popular through his television program, the *700 Club*. He used its success to become the head of a profitable media company (its most valuable asset was the Family Channel), which he eventually sold to the media baron Rupert Murdoch for close to $2 billion. (Like Falwell, Robertson is also involved in higher education; his Regent University in Virginia Beach aims at being a first-rate institution with graduate schools in communications and law.)

Aside from his religious broadcasting, Robertson is perhaps best known for his run in the 1988 Republican presidential primary. An early strong showing in Michigan during the spring of 1988, thanks to a good organization, strong finances, and media expertise, suggested that evangelicals were beginning to make political inroads not simply by generating support for established candidates but by nurturing politicians of their own. But as Robertson's campaign played out it showed almost the reverse and confirmed the collapse of the Moral Majority. No one expected Robertson to beat Vice President George Bush for the Republican nomination. But it was surprising to see how evangelicals like Falwell abandoned Robertson for Bush. Part of the problem may have been theological. Robertson was a charismatic evangelical whose beliefs about special private revelations from the Holy Spirit alienated other evangelicals who held that divine revelation was limited to the Bible. During the year before the campaign a number of televangelists had been caught in financial and sexual scandals, further damaging Robertson's reputation as a religious broadcaster even though his own personal affairs were in good order. Yet another factor in Robertson's failed campaign was the relatively narrow appeal of the issues that energized evangelicals. These Protestants did confront a society where their concerns for Christian families and children were being challenged in schools, the media, and the courts. But these concerns did not make for a successful political platform that would enlist a reliable majority of voters. Aside from the lack of a coherent set of policies on domestic and international issues, the moral agenda of evangelicals was doomed to look judgmental and selfish. The treatment Robertson received from the media, along with his own failures, exposed the limited appeal of morality as a political platform.

Robertson's experience in the 1988 presidential primaries may explain the most recent manifestation of evangelical political activities, the Christian Coalition. Founded in 1989 by Robertson, the organization in effect picked up where the

Moral Majority left off. Its aim is to promote Christian values in public life and give Christians a voice in American politics. Although the Coalition's rhetoric may use the word "family" less frequently, its outlook is like that of LaHaye and his goal of sending "pro-moral" elected officials to Washington. The organization also promotes political involvement in local politics, striving to establish a grassroots organizational base while continuing to rank national candidates according to a strict set of moral guidelines.

As much as the Christian Coalition resembles the Moral Majority, it also reflects a growing awareness—even on the part of Robertson—that evangelicals need to strike a less self-righteous public posture if they are going to gain a wider hearing. This recognition may account for the person whom Robertson chose to direct the Christian Coalition, Ralph Reed. A young man of twenty-eight years, fresh from a Ph.D. in American history at Emory University, Reed at the time was an unlikely choice. But he had been active as an undergraduate in Republican student organizations and had founded Students for America, thus displaying an ability for the kind of network building necessary for establishing the Coalition. Reed was especially well suited for the new organization's first priority—enlisting members. He did so by targeting controversial works of art funded by the National Endowment for the Arts, such as the creations of Andres Serrano and Robert Mapplethorpe. Although some people construed these as attacks on free speech and artistic integrity, they proved to be a successful strategy for generating money and members. By 1991 the Coalition had 82,000 members, was financially secure, and could take partial credit for helping reelect North Carolina Senator Jesse Helms through its mass distribution of voter guides to that state's citizens.

By 1992, however, with George Bush's defeat the worst of any incumbent since 1912, the effectiveness of the Coalition looked questionable. Clearly Reed had built an organization that could mobilize voters nationally and locally. But was the moral agenda of evangelical politics the basis for a national coalition beyond born-again Protestants? One answer came in 1994 when Republicans gained control of Congress for the first time in forty years, running on their "Contract with America," with significant input from Reed and the Christian Coalition. Interestingly, that contract did not refer to promoral issues such as abortion or funding for the National Endowment for the Arts. One answer, then, was that for evangelicals to have a substantial role even in conservative political causes they would have to back away from biblical morality.

Reed himself elaborated on the question of whether evangelicalism provided a basis for governance in his 1996 book, *Active Faith*. His aim was to explain and justify the religious right and the Christian Coalition. Aside from his account of the Coalition's history and mission, what stands out is his effort to portray evangelicals in a moderate light. For example, he quotes approvingly the mainline Protestant theologian Reinhold Niebuhr, Mother Theresa, Pope John Paul II, and Martin Luther King, Jr., in part to show that the religious right shares the concerns of nonevangelicals. In itself, this feature of the book demonstrated a political pragmatism that was not evident in an earlier generation of evangelicals engaged in American public life. Yet Reed also showed that the pro-family and pro-moral agenda that had energized evangelicals in the late 1960s remained the dominant theme of the movement's political leaders. In a revealing passage he tried to argue that political compromise did not necessarily lead to ethical concessions:

> The broadening of our issues focus, however, has sometimes created the mistaken impression that we are less con-

cerned with the moral issues that many associate with the pro-family movement. Nothing could be farther from the truth.... The pro-family movement has likewise learned that restricting abortion and battling homosexuality alone do not help families pay their bills, send their children to college, or save for retirement. When the pro-family movement talks about lower taxes or job security, we are not trying to hide our "true agenda," as some critics insist. We are simply addressing both the moral and the financial pressures on so many families today.

As Reed's reflections suggest, since the 1960s evangelicals had in some ways become wiser about the rules governing American politics. But as his book also shows, they had not moved very far beyond a political agenda defined by the moral imperatives upholding the middle-class American family. Part of the evangelical commitment to family values can be explained by the changes in the United States that made those values less attractive, and by the political leverage that these issues gave conservative political candidates and organizers. But it also reflected the direct application of evangelicalism's concern for godly living to issues of public life. For many evangelicals, the way they thought of their own quest for holiness was also the way that they ended up thinking about society. This is why it is a mistake to conclude that evangelicalism's focus on soul-winning automatically results in a socially withdrawn or passive faith. The activities of the religious right prove the opposite. The moral strenuousness of evangelical piety ordinarily invites born-again Protestants to demand of society the same sort of righteousness they expect from one another.

To conclude that Tim LaHaye, Jerry Falwell, Pat Robertson, the Moral Majority, or the Christian Coalition represent the political views of all evangelicals would be a mistake. Mistaken too would be the notion that moral issues alone motivate evangelicals in the public arena. Too often the first word in the phrase "religious right" obscures the second, causing students of evangelical politics to miss the obvious point that born-again Protestants are generally conservative politically. As much as preserving the family has given evangelicals a voice in debates about public policy, their political leaders have shared with other conservatives a commitment to democracy, small government, free markets, and the United States' responsibility to promote these ideals around the world. For many evangelicals these conservative political convictions were a given and needed little emphasis compared to public morality and policies affecting the family. That Southern evangelicals would emerge as spokesmen for these political principles is not particularly startling, since the South has been and continues to be a source of political and cultural conservatism. Consequently the emergence of the religious right should not be severed from the post-1980 resurgence of political conservatism generally.

At the same time not every evangelical identifies with political conservatism. In the same year (1996) that Ralph Reed's book *Active Faith* appeared, Jim Wallis responded with *Who Speaks for God?* The subtitle of Wallis's book—*An Alternative to the Religious Right*—spoke volumes. The founding editor of *Sojourners* magazine, who came of age politically during the late 1960s as an opponent of the Vietnam War and the status quo in American race relations, Wallis has been a leader among a left-leaning group of evangelicals committed to social justice. His 1996 book was no less than a call for biblically based politics and moral reflection on matters of social importance. But Wallis believed that Reed, Robertson, and the Christian Coalition did not speak for all evangelicals, nor did they expound a genuinely religious perspective on public life. Instead, Wallis argued, the religious right had been "hijacked" by political conservatives, and in the process evangelicalism had been reduced to ideology, not the prophetic voice clearly articulated in Scripture. His alternative was a politics of compassion, community, and civility, one that transcended the partisanship of left and right and that would morally invigorate American society in the same way that antebellum Northern evangelicals had once opposed slavery, extended suffrage, and protected children.

Wallis and Reed may have disagreed about politics, but in the end evangelicals, whether left or right, thought about American society and government in remarkably similar ways. Both sought to reclaim the United States' evangelical heritage, and both believed that faith needed to be recovered at a time when American society was turning secular. Each man also thought he was speaking for the disfranchised, Wallis for the underclass and Reed for believers who had been neglected by mainstream politicians. Throughout most of the twentieth century many Americans had thought of evangelicals primarily for their talents at soul-winning and revivalism. But in the end, as much as evangelical Protestantism gained adherents by promising the rewards of eternal life, Wallis and Reed showed how much born-again Protestants would not be content with a private faith but instead believed the gospel to be remarkably relevant to public life.

6

Evangelicals and Popular Culture

IN 1997 the Southern Baptist Convention (SBC) at its annual national meeting passed a resolution against The Disney Company. The specific wording went as follows: the messengers of the SBC "urge every Southern Baptist to take the stewardship of their time, money, and resources so seriously that they refrain from patronizing The Disney Company and any of its related entities, understanding that this is not an attempt to bring The Disney Company down, but to bring Southern Baptists up to the moral standard of God." The resolution went on to indicate that Southern Baptists should use similar reasons for avoiding the goods and services of other companies, because Disney alone was not guilty of "promoting immoral ideologies such as homosexuality, infidelity, and adultery." The SBC also pointed out that its leadership had been in correspondence with executives at Disney who refused to address the Southern Baptists' concern, and that the Convention had been deliberating this action for several years. In other words, the SBC had no vendetta against Disney and this action did not come out of the blue. But it nonetheless was a church ruling rich in irony. Here was the largest Protestant denomination in the United States, with more than fifteen million members, a church known for its conservative teaching and practice, condemning the company that had given America one of its most wholesome icons, Mickey Mouse. For some the SBC's decision reflected a fundamentalist mentality so intent on a separate moral purity that even motherhood, baseball, and apple pie could appear worldly.

At one level the SBC's resolution against Disney reflects an ongoing antagonism between evangelicalism and worldliness. Over the last three decades of the twentieth century, Southern Baptists had played out their own rendition of the earlier fundamentalist controversy. During the 1970s the denomination divided fairly neatly into two camps, the so-called fundamentalists and the so-called moderates. The former insisted upon the inerrancy of the Bible while the latter responded with the Southern Baptist doctrine of soul liberty, an idea that most often involved intellectual liberty. By the 1990s the conservative party had gained control of the SBC, a reversal of what had happened in the fundamentalist controversy of the 1920s. With that fundamentalist victory, the SBC demonstrated its evangelical identity by reaffirming a theologically conservative statement of faith, urging its members to avoid the products of Disney and declaring that wives, in accordance with biblical teaching, should submit "graciously" to their husbands. Although Southern Baptists themselves are uncomfortable with the term "evangelical"—a word some think has too many Yankee connotations—most observers of American Protestantism look to the SBC as evidence of where evangelical teachings inevitably lead—opposition to moral relativism and liberalism, both political and theological.

Regarding the SBC's resolution against Disney as further evidence of evangelical hostility to mainstream American culture is not the only possible interpretation. For at the same time Southern Baptists heard this verdict from the messengers they sent to the annual convention, they were Americans who were consuming large quantities of popular culture without the discernment that Southern Baptist leaders believed necessary. The declaration against Disney, then, was both an indication of evangelical morality and a sign of how acculturated evangelicals had become. One reason for this acculturation was evangelicals' knack for using mass media for religious ends, a talent that also cultivated a taste for popular entertainment, whether produced by executives at Disney or the Billy Graham Evangelistic Association.

Here it is important to reiterate that evangelicals came to prominence during the 1970s through a sophisticated use of television programming. Jerry Falwell's *Old Fashioned Revival Hour* and Pat Robertson's *700 Club* enabled their hosts to gain a national audience that soon attracted the attention of Republican strategists who were looking for ways to recruit support for conservative political candidates. During the 1980s evangelicals continued to attract attention, though this time negative, through the medium of television. First in 1988, Jimmy Swaggart, a minister in the Assemblies of God, was discovered to have been involved with a New Orleans prostitute despite his own heated denunciations of adultery and sexual immorality on the air. Then, a year later, Jim and Tammy Bakker, the hosts of the popular *Praise the Lord* telecast, were convicted of fraud and tax evasion in their schemes to build a religious resort that ironically was modeled after Disney World. These developments—first the rise to political prominence of Falwell and Robertson, followed by Swaggart's and the Bakkers' fall from grace—fixed in the minds of many Americans that evangelicalism's leaders were hypocrites, using religion for partisan politics or as cover for sinful pleasures.

As destructive as these images were for televangelists, they obscured a far more important feature of evangelicalism. TV preachers such as Falwell, Robertson, Swaggart, and Bakker were simply one part of a much larger presence of born-again Protestants in the electronic media and popular culture. Ever since the revivals of the First Great Awakening in colonial

America, evangelicals had shown an ability for exploiting new communications technology and business practices to advance religion. Throughout the twentieth century this pattern continued, first with radio and then with television. Evangelicals have always been on watch for forms of communication that can reach as many people as possible with the message of the Bible. In the second half of the twentieth century, born-again Protestants expanded their repertoire with ventures into media that involved much more than preaching. They blossomed into highly profitable forms of entertainment.

The evangelical activities that had once formed the backbone of a religious subculture had isolated these Protestants from the temptations of worldliness. But after 1970 these activities emerged as a cultural expression that could appeal to Americans who were not themselves identifiably evangelical. In itself this shift from the sidelines to the cultural mainstream demonstrated that evangelicals were much more prosperous and comfortable with their place in American society than a previous generation had been, thus partly accounting for their entrance into politics as a way to protect and consolidate their gains. But equally important is what evangelical popular culture reveals about this particular form of Protestantism: as much as people perceive evangelicalism as old-fashioned and conservative, it has actually been one of the most modern and innovative forms of Christianity in using the cultural vernacular to restate the claims of an ancient faith in a modern tongue.

James Dobson's radio broadcast *Focus on the Family* is now the leading daily syndicated religious program in the United States, a position it has held for over a decade. Dobson's show, which usually features interviews with guests about a variety of family issues, is carried by more than 2,500 stations in 95 countries and 6 different languages. Despite his international audience, the listeners that matter most to Dobson are those residing in the United States, a country that according to him has lost its moral bearings. A trained psychologist with a Ph.D. in child development from the University of Southern California, Dobson first came to prominence with *Dare to Discipline* (1970), a book that counseled parents on the best (read: biblical) way to rear children. This title, along with several others written during the early 1970s, became best-sellers and established Dobson as the evangelical equivalent of Dr. Spock. Eventually the demand for Dobson's folksy advice became so great that he decided to launch a radio broadcast. The timing of this initiative was fortuitous. Dobson's message about the moral breakdown of American society and his focus on the family as an institution to right America's decadence coincided with the rise of the religious right. It added to his psychological advice the urgency of social and political reform. No wonder, then, that a man who started out dispensing biblically informed psychological recommendations about the relations between parents and children, and husbands and wives, would eventually become one of the most powerful members of the religious right. Evidence of Dobson's political effectiveness was on display, for instance, in 1992 when he devoted one of his broadcasts to a legislative initiative in Colorado, the home of *Focus on the Family*, that would have nullified gay rights legislation. Although the United States Supreme Court eventually struck down the measure as unconstitutional, Dobson's support for it was crucial to the legislation's success in a statewide referendum.

Episodes like Colorado's battle over gay rights, or Dobson's 1998 threat to leave the Republican party because it had abandoned family values, have attracted the most attention from political commentators and media analysts. But although the *Focus on the Family* radio show is the engine that pulls the rest of Dobson's endeavors, it is only one part of a multifaceted corporation that says as much about evangelical attitudes toward culture as it does about the religious right. For at the same time Dobson advises parents on the best way to rear disciplined children, or exhorts congressmen to pass family-friendly legislation, he also oversees a company that employs a vast array of writers, editors, and videomakers to create and monitor wholesome entertainment for evangelical parents and children.

A recent trip to the *Focus on the Family* website, for instance, revealed feature stories for each segment of the evangelical family. Parents could read a story about Islam that tried to make sense of the September 11, 2001, terrorist attacks on the World Trade Center and the Pentagon. In its "Husbands and Wives" section, a female writer gave women tips on football, with definitions of such key terms as "defense" and "extra point," so that wives could participate in some credible way with their spouses' enjoyment of the Super Bowl. For college students, *Focus on the Family* posted an article about grandparents and the way Americans often neglect to care for and learn from the elderly. For teenagers the website had another article about Super Bowl Sunday, this time with a twist. It featured a group of teens from a Sunday school class in Columbia, South Carolina, who used the annual championship of the National Football League to hold Souper Bowl Sunday, a day devoted to feeding the homeless and hungry in their city. Finally, the children's section featured a variety of short jokes, submitted by boys and girls in the *Focus on the Family* audience, such as the following: "Q. What did the digital clock say to its mother? A. Look ma, no hands."

These examples suggest at least three notable features about Dobson's work on behalf of the family. First, *Focus on the Family* functions as much more than the political lobby that generates the most media attention. Second, the organization segments its audience into age groups that form the basis for its various products. Finally, as a clearinghouse of timely in-

formation about American popular culture and a producer itself of family-oriented culture, *Focus on the Family* reveals a
side of evangelical Protestantism that is fully assimilated to
mainstream American society. As opposed to the era when
many born-again Protestants would have raised questions
about violating the Sabbath by watching sports on television,
or criticized as worldly the halftime entertainment during the
Super Bowl, *Focus on the Family* appears to baptize rather
than reject American popular culture.

One way that *Focus on the Family* illustrates evangelicalism's growing acceptance of mainstream culture, despite its
political protests about immorality, is in the guidance it offers
parents about motion pictures, television, and contemporary
music. An earlier generation of evangelicals had shunned such
products as worldly, "of the devil" being a phrase some ministers would use. They had no time for advice about what to
view or see from America's entertainment industry. But rather
than counseling parents to avoid various amusements for the
sake of considering more spiritual and heavenly fare, *Focus on
the Family* reviews of popular culture indicate—much like the
SBC's stand against Disney—an evangelical audience that is
fully conversant with mainstream popular culture. They also
indicate that the main reason for reviewing film, television,
and music is the health of the family; parents need to be able to
monitor what their children watch and hear, not whether the
latest Hollywood hit is aesthetically worthwhile. For instance,
in its review of *A Beautiful Mind*, the 2002 Academy Award
winner for best picture, starring Russell Crowe as a schizo-
phrenic mathematician who eventually wins the Nobel Prize,
Focus on the Family gives the picture high marks for the lead
character's faithfulness as a husband, his devotion as an uncle,
and his disciplined work ethic. But it goes on to document the
film's sexual content, violence, crude language ("Two dozen
profanities include several s-words and 10 misuses of God's

name [five are exclamations of Jesus' name]"), and its characters' use of alcohol and drugs. In the end, though, the review praises the movie for its thoughtful story and faults Hollywood for always having to add foul language and sexual immorality to spice up an otherwise valuable film.

Focus on the Family offers similar advice to parents about music and television programming. The review of Britney Spears's CD *Britney*, for example, continues to evaluate along the family-sensitive lines of foul language and sexual innuendo. On the plus side, the performer receives credit for admitting in the song "I'm Not a Girl, Not Yet a Woman," that she doesn't have the answers to "everything." But her use of profanity to show her independence, along with the sexual themes of the songs "I'm a Slave 4 U" and "Anticipating," lead the *Focus on the Family* reviewer to conclude that Spears "uses sleazy outfits, sensual themes and occasional profanity to prove [convincingly] she's not a little girl anymore." A review of Backstreet Boys' CD *Black & Blue* judges according to the same moral grid. The Boys gain points for intimating long-term romantic relationships in the songs "Yes I Will," "I Promise You with Everything I Am," and "How Did I Ever Fall in Love with You." But the group ends up disappointing when in "The Call" it alludes to cheating on one of these long-term relationships, and when in "Shining Star" it suggests "physical intimacy" with a romantic partner. On the whole, the review gives the CD a grade of a B+ on musical criteria, but a D- on "moral judgment." It also notes that although the Backstreet Boys offer music that is appealing to teens and does not alienate parents, an interview with *Rolling Stone* undermines the group's credibility by photographing its members with nude women and revealing that they have engaged in such "immoral habits" as "cohabitation, cussing, going to strip clubs."

Focus on the Family also keeps close tabs on television, offering parents evaluations of the networks' most popular shows. Its review of *Malcolm in the Middle* is predictable given the organization's commitment to family values and the program's portrayal of family life as inherently dysfunctional. The show clearly reflects "real life," but it goes "too far" by ridiculing "organized religion," endorsing "bad behavior," and reinforcing TV's "modern family mantra: *parents are stupid*." Not even "a few cheap laughs and half-hearted moral lessons" could justify exposing children to such an outlook. The review of *Will & Grace,* a TV show with the implicit message that homosexuality is normal, also offers few surprises. "The Scriptures strongly disagree" with the notion that being gay is no big deal. At the same time the reviewer wants to be clear that opposition to gay rights is not a reason for hating homosexuals. Even so, parents have little reason for allowing children to watch the show. In the end, the best bets on television are game shows like *Who Wants to Be a Millionaire*. Of course, the questions that Regis Philbin asks are "dumbed down" compared to *Jeopardy*. But game shows provide families with the chance to sit down together and watch and learn "without fear of indecent exposure."

The impression clearly communicated by *Focus on the Family*'s assessment of popular culture—one shared by many evangelicals if the popularity of Dobson and his radio broadcast is any indication—is that contemporary born-again Protestants, unlike their grandparents, are unwilling to be culturally separate. Instead they want a sanitized version of the most popular forms of entertainment. As these sample reviews also suggest, evangelicals who worry about rearing moral and guileless children will have trouble finding movies, television programming, and music that is wholesome. In response, *Focus on the Family* has produced radio programming and videos for children and radio theater for families that are designed to be reliable conduits of evangelicalism's moral teaching.

Adventures in Odyssey is the most visible of the organization's efforts in family entertainment. The series began in 1986 when Dobson sought an alternative form of Saturday-morning cartoons for children between the ages of eight and twelve. A year later a pilot series aired for thirteen weeks, and the response from listeners was so favorable that *Focus on the Family* made *Adventures* a staple of its various activities. The thirty-minute radio show airs nightly on almost two thousand stations, often before Dobson's own broadcast, and are modeled on the sort of dramatic programming heard during the "Golden Age" of radio. A video series has also spun off from the radio program. The stories are set in a fictional small town called Odyssey and feature plots and characters that attempt to show the relevance of biblical teaching to the particular struggles of the town's Christian families. The first twelve videos provide a good sample of the kinds of issues that the series addresses. Each episode comes with Scripture references and a theme. The topics include: "Materialism versus Lasting Treasure," "Loving Your Neighbor," "Responsibility and the Consequences," "Faithfulness to Friends and God," "Teamwork," "Kindness and Brotherly Love," "The True Meaning of Christmas," "Keeping Your Word," "God's Sovereignty," "Seeing Other's Through God's Eyes," "You Will Reap What You Sow," and "Be Careful What You Let in Your Mind."

Although these themes are fairly conventional for white, middle-class families in the United States, they are also religiously generic. Except for the videos on Christmas and divine sovereignty, the rest could safely appeal to nonevangelical parents who want their offspring to be decent and honorable citizens. Even in their treatment of matters of doctrinal importance, these videos end up stressing morality and how believers are supposed to behave rather than the nature of God and the contents of the Bible. For instance, in the story about Christmas the narrative reveals a boy who is so intent on winning a contest for a new bicycle that he treats shabbily a friend and a less fortunate boy in the neighborhood who have also entered the contest. When the main character loses the contest but still is given the bike he doesn't deserve by the winner of the competition, a friend who constructed a simple display that reflected the spiritual nature of Christmas, he realizes that the birth of Christ teaches the same lesson—that God gave humankind a gift it did not deserve.

Adventures in Odyssey reveals the other side of evangelicalism's promotion of family values. While Dobson can rally his listeners to call members of Congress when a particular piece of legislation affects families, his political activism is only one part of the equation, and perhaps not even the largest element. Evangelical organizations such as *Focus on the Family* are devoted to protecting and advancing families as the primary agent of socialization. Helping parents in the rearing of godly and responsible children is the main task. This suggests that only when public institutions pose a barrier to parents' responsibilities do evangelicals turn from cultivating warm and moral climates in the private sphere of the home to lobbying public officials in the public sphere of the legislature.

Focus on the Family's line of children's videos, combined with its monitoring of America's entertainment industry, nicely represents how evangelicals began to approach popular culture after years of being secluded in a religious ghetto. In many ways the phenomenal popularity of the organization's programming reflects born-again Protestantism's ingenuity for packaging Christianity in sophisticated technology as well as its interest in mass forms of communication. Just as evangelicals were among the first American Protestants in the twentieth century to recognize the importance of radio, so Dobson and his associates are continuing the search for the most popular forms of media (evangelicals typically equate popularity with effectiveness, at least because of the size of the potential audience). Just as Paul Rader and Charles Fuller introduced radio programs whose appeal derived in part from more entertaining elements such as contemporary gospel music, rather than preaching alone, so *Focus on the Family* continues to attract audiences by forms of communication that are decidedly different from those experienced in church. The appeal of evangelical media productions is that they have a biblical focus and thus attract believers who want to be edified. At the same time, unlike the sermons delivered by the average evangelical pastor each week, the biblical content of evangelical family programming is ironically meager. The story or the interview with the featured guest ends up being the central feature, not the Bible.

As much as *Focus on the Family* continues evangelicalism's history of media savvy, it also represents a shift in emphasis within born-again Protestantism's understanding of and contribution to American popular culture. Before the late 1970s, even though evangelicals showed great skill in finding new ways to use mass communication, the primary purpose of such endeavors was basically evangelistic. Evangelical preachers and ministries were dedicated to making new converts, and radio, televised mass rallies, and cheap publications appeared to be an effective way of reaching large numbers of unbelievers. In many ways Billy Graham was a pioneer in finding alternative forms for communicating the evangelical message. Shortly after he gained the national spotlight with his Los Angeles crusade in 1949, he formed World Wide Pictures, a motion picture company designed to produce Hollywood-style movies that would inspire and attract converts. The company's first commercial success came in 1965 with *The Restless Ones*, a movie released in first-run theaters around the nation. Its star was the actor Johnny Crawford, whom many television viewers knew as the boy who played the son of *The Rifle*

Man. The movie actually foreshadowed the kind of story that *Focus on the Family* videos and radio theater would eventually feature: a boy suffering various temptations, whose faith was the turning point in resolving the crisis. In *The Restless Ones* the particular temptations were sex and drugs, themes a bit racier than the children's fare portrayed in *Focus on the Family* dramas. But in addition to demonstrating the victory that comes through faith, the film also provided parents with a vehicle through which they might communicate with their children on difficult subjects.

Another important evangelical venture into motion pictures was the movie *A Thief in the Night* (1973). This film did not reach first-run theaters, but since its release it has been one of the most popular films ever seen by evangelical audiences. *Thief* tells the story of a couple, one of whom converts, who are alive at the end of history, and how horrible life is once Christians are taken up to meet Christ (what dispensationalists call the "rapture"). The fantastic nature of the story gives the movie a genuinely science-fiction feel that makes for a scary plot. In addition to turning evangelical theology about Christ's second coming into an enthralling movie, *Thief* also became popular among born-again Protestants because it lent itself to evangelistic uses. The film begins and ends with the same sequence of events, at first raising questions that the story goes on to answer, later showing what happens to those who will not convert. The movie has literally scared the hell out of those who converted after viewing it. This may explain why the movie has been translated and dubbed into three foreign languages and supplied with subtitles for numerous other nations. It is a noteworthy example of evangelicals employing technology and entertainment media to seek converts.

The same emphasis can be seen in Jerry Falwell's popular television program, *The Old Time Gospel Hour* (a broadcast named after Charles Fuller's popular 1940s radio broadcast,

The Old Fashioned Revival Hour). As in the case of James Dobson, Falwell's television show preceded his entrance into political activism, and the Virginia pastor's leadership within the religious right would not have been possible had it not been for the large viewing audience, at one time estimated at 25 million. Unlike evangelical movies, *The Old Time Gospel Hour* is not necessarily the most captivating television. It is simply a recording of the Sunday morning worship service at Falwell's Baptist church in Lynchburg, Virginia, edited to fit a sixty-minute time slot. Of course it features close-ups of Falwell and the singers who perform during the service, and the telecast includes a split-screen shot of a person communicating the verbal content of the program in sign language for the hearing impaired. But the aim of the broadcast is much like *The Restless Ones* and *A Thief in the Night*: to communicate the message of evangelical Christianity and win new converts. In other words, the religious intentions on the show are explicit; it is designed to evangelize, not simply to provide alternative forms of television for the evangelical audience.

The uses to which evangelicals could put the media of popular culture began to expand in the case of Pat Robertson, another evangelical leader who used his communications empire as a springboard to politics. In 1986 he appeared on the cover of *Time* magazine as the United States' leading "televangelist." But Robertson was not really an evangelist who used television. His popular broadcast, the *700 Club*, was the first evangelical television program to introduce the talk-show format. Robertson, with his master-of-ceremonies sidekick, would parade before millions of viewers various personalities for a discussion of the most pressing issues of the day (over time these issues took on a decidedly political theme). Robertson's *700 Club* apparently breeds the same kind of intimacy between the host and viewers that many daytime television watchers sense with Regis Philbin or Oprah Winfrey.

Although Robertson was not the first broadcaster to begin to blur the lines between religious programming and entertainment with religious themes, he was the evangelical leader who began to do for television what Dobson was doing in a much smaller way with radio theater and its video spinoff. Oral Roberts, a popular Assemblies of God minister from Oklahoma, in 1968 pioneered in producing prime-time specials that featured believing entertainers in a variety show format. But Robertson was one of the first broadcasters to expand the horizons of religious television on a daily basis, thus raising the possibility of producing round-the-clock programming for evangelical audiences *only*. His intent was not first to evangelize but to provide an alternative to the mainstream entertainment industry. Even more significant was Robertson's sense of an audience that desired safe alternatives to network television shows. In 1989 the parent company that produced *700 Club* changed its name from the Christian Broadcasting Network (CBN) to the Family Channel and began to broadcast not only religious programming but also popular television shows from the 1960s, such as *Father Knows Best*, and *Leave It to Beaver*, programs thought to be uplifting and family-oriented forms of entertainment, even if not overtly Christian.

If Robertson's foray into religious television has broken down barriers that once restricted the evangelical use of the entertainment media to the winning of new converts, the hugely successful novels of Frank Peretti and the team of Tim LaHaye and Jerry Jenkins have transformed the dramatic story of the second coming from an evangelistic tool into a series of best-sellers. In the 1980s Peretti, a relatively obscure but productive writer living in the Pacific Northwest, came to prominence with his novels *The Present Darkness* (1986) and *Piercing the Darkness* (1989), both of which were Christian best-sellers well into the 1990s. Peretti's fiction features the drama of biblical prophecy set in small-town America. His novels' appeal stems in part from the way in which they transport the everyday affairs of average Americans into the cosmic conflict between angels and demons. In addition to keeping alive evangelical interest in the end times, Peretti's books also play to born-again Protestant suspicions about secular humanism and its pervasive, if not conspiratorial, influence upon American society. The battle between the forces of darkness and light is not simply one between spiritual beings but involves the daily conflict across America between God-fearing and God-denying officials and citizens. After the initial success of his first two books, Peretti followed with *Prophet* (1992) and *The Oath* (1995). These novels did not sell as well as the first two, in part because other evangelicals were soon flooding the market with fictional renderings about Christ's return and the end of history.

Of the other works of fiction based on biblical prophecy (Pat Robertson even entered the field with *The End of the Age* [1995]), the *Left Behind* series by Tim LaHaye and Jerry Jenkins is the most successful. In some ways the series is amazing if only for displaying the range of LaHaye's career—from a conservative pastor in southern California who in the 1960s became something of a political activist, to a prodigious writer during the 1970s and 1980s on family, cultural, and biblical topics, to the author of a wildly popular fiction series that apparently has as many spin-off lines of merchandise and spiritual counsel as *Focus on the Family*. The series began in 1995 with the first novel, *Left Behind: A Novel of the Earth's Last Days*, and continued apace with a little more than one sequel per year. With the 2001 publication of *Desecration: AntiChrist Takes the Throne*, LaHaye and Jenkins had produced 9 books with no end in sight, thanks to the more than 40 million copies sold. (*Desecration* itself had a 2.9 million first printing, the largest for any hardcover novel published in 2001, and the next in the series, *The Remnant*, is scheduled at the time of this writing for a July 2002 release and a $3 million publicity budget.) Like the movie *A Thief in the Night*, which featured the song from which LaHaye and Jenkins take the title of their series, "You've Been Left Behind," these novels are based upon what happens on earth after Christ returns and Christians are raptured up into heaven. Chaos breaks out as wicked rulers attempt world dominance while a remnant church of believers who figure out the Bible's meaning battle against the forces of evil. The *Left Behind* series shows not only evangelicals' entrepreneurial instincts but also how easily the dispensationalist interpretation of the Bible that gave evangelicalism a measure of coherence from 1900 to 1970 can be turned into highly entertaining science fiction. The series was so captivating that in 2000 and 2001 it spawned a video and movie that earned more than $4 million—though LaHaye eventually sued the producer for not making it even more successful.

In many respects these novels by LaHaye, Jenkins, and Peretti (and there are many evangelical writers in this genre) are simply riding the coattails of biblical prophecy's seemingly endless appeal to American mass markets. Hal Lindsey's *Late Great Planet Earth* (1970), a book about the unfolding of biblical prophecy in international affairs that raised fears of another world war, was the nonfiction best-seller of the 1970s, with 9 million copies in print by 1978 and 28 million by 1990. Statistics such as these—and Lindsey's book was the most successful on an already crowded shelf—indicate that an appetite for millennialism already existed before creative writers combined evangelical theology with the entertainment values of science fiction. Where Peretti and novelists like him have been innovative is in expanding material once reserved for prophecy conferences, Bible studies, and evangelism into characters and plots for a form of amusement and diversion. This is not to say that evangelical readers who make these novels best-sellers are simply reading for escape. Part of the success of these books can be attributed to their promise of spiritual edification. But now, in addition to the serious aim of confirming devout readers in the truths of the Bible, evangelical fiction also represents a pious form of recreation that entertains.

The cumulative effect of evangelical forays into radio, television, motion pictures, and popular fiction has been to highlight a subtle ambiguity in born-again Protestantism that makes it appealing to popular audiences at the same time it reinforces cultural separatism. One of the striking aspects of evangelical cultural expressions is how personal their plots and subject matter tend to be. From the *Focus on the Family* radio theater, with its characters whose faith is tested and who learn the moral of the story, to Frank Peretti's novels, which explore the plight of believers after the return of Christ, evangelical stories revel in the individual's religious experience. This tendency in evangelical popular culture is natural, given the importance of conversion. Born-again Protestantism is primarily a religion of the heart, and it stresses the subjective experience of the convert and his or her spiritual struggles.

During the middle decades of the twentieth century, when evangelicals thrived within their own religious subculture, the movement's priority was evangelism. Evangelical radio shows, television, movies, and books were geared explicitly toward making new converts. But these cultural expressions were not simply filled with quotations and stories from the Bible. In fact, many of the most effective evangelical ministries relied upon the personal experiences of converts whose stories moved nonbelievers to convert. Nevertheless the point of telling a story, whether individually at a church rally or in a movie, was to win more people to Christ.

This approach began to change during the 1970s and 1980s with the recognition that the conversion experience and trials of faith provided not only emotionally charged material for producing converts. The personal lives of believers also made moving subject matter for reading and viewing pleasure. The telling of evangelical stories of faith, whether in print, on the radio, or on the screen, thus became an alternative form of entertainment for believers concerned about the immorality and secular humanism that filled television programming and Hollywood movies. In effect the production values that evangelicals learned in using mass media to communicate the message of their faith to large audiences became part of a winning strategy for creating an evangelical entertainment industry. Of course, because the content of evangelical broadcasts and publications is often the same whether designed for conversion or edification, authors, producers, and directors can fall back on evangelism as a justification. Nevertheless the expansion of evangelical media during the 1970s and 1980s to include entertainment as much as evangelism indicates the dual uses of the evangelical interest in the personal lives of converts. As a result, the line dividing evangelicalism as a form of entertainment and a means of gaining new converts has become harder and harder to detect.

If evangelical novels, movies, and television illustrate the reemergence of born-again Protestantism from its cultural isolation to be a thriving and popular form of faith, the Contemporary Christian Music (CCM) industry confirms the point that within evangelicalism the difference between religion and entertainment is becoming indistinct. Before 1970, evangelicals had many favorite musicians and songwriters, from George Beverly Shea, a baritone soloist who sang old-time gospel hymns and songs at Billy Graham's crusades, to Ralph Carmichael, a songwriter and arranger who wrote the score for Billy Graham's film *The Restless Ones* and arranged choral and instrumental music for churches. Their music,

however, was designed primarily for evangelical audiences in
religious settings, such as worship, church concerts, or evangelistic rallies. Around 1970, however, evangelical music began
to change in the same ways that evangelical movies, television,
and novels were changing—from a tool for evangelism to a
competitor in the popular music industry.

Evangelical music altered dramatically in 1969 when Capi-
tol Records released the album *I Love You* by Larry Norman,
considered to be the first "Jesus rock" artist. Norman grew up
in San Jose, California, and had been part of a band called
People. But when he decided upon a solo career and a major
record company signed him to a contract, he emerged immediately, in the words of the *New York Times*, as "Christian
rock's most intelligent writer and greatest asset." Among the
most memorable of Norman's songs was one that summed up
well the outlook of this new phenomenon of Christian rock,
"Why Should the Devil Have All the Good Music?" One of
the verses reads: "I want the people to know that he saved my
soul / But I still like to listen to the radio / They say 'rock and
roll is wrong, we'll give you one more chance' / I say I feel so
good I gotta get up and dance."

The rise of CCM depended heavily on the evangelical
segment of the post–World War II baby boom. The generation sometimes described as "Woodstock," "Pepsi," "Rock,"
"Protest," or "Me," was idealistic and affluent, compared to
previous ones, and its members took part in the variety of
protest movements against which evangelical leaders would
reassert the family and enter the public arena. While an older
generation of evangelicals sought to undo the social and cultural effects of the 1960s, many of their children were caught
in the middle, sympathizing with the idealism of their peers
and yet holding on in some measure to the born-again faith.
These evangelical teens and young adults formed the backbone of the Jesus Movement, a loose collection of activists,

youth ministers, entertainers, and born-again hippies who viewed a more relaxed brand of evangelicalism as providing the solution to the various ills dividing America. Jesus Rock embodied the kind of Christianity the Jesus People thought Americans needed to believe: it was hip *and* biblical. Like other forms of evangelical culture, this music's design was evangelistic, but it ended up providing a safe alternative for evangelicals who wanted to join the youth culture of the 1970s but knew their beliefs placed limits on their association.

The older generation of evangelicals did not offer a warm reception to the Jesus People and their music, and this prompted creative strategies for overcoming the opposition. Protestant church leaders in both evangelical and mainline congregations regarded rock and roll as a form of protest, laced with drugs and sex, against decency and wholesomeness. The idea of using it to communicate a Christian message appeared to be naive. At the same time the musicians who produced Christian rock had difficulty reaching audiences larger than Jesus festivals and coffeehouses. Christian broadcasters had not yet segmented religious radio according to age and gender, thus leaving evangelical radio in the early 1970s in the hands of preachers and Bible expositors. But Christian record companies saw a potential market and began to sign Jesus rockers to contracts, and the publicity and distribution of records created a wider audience for the new evangelical music. Early favorites were the singers Randy Matthews and Andre Crouch, and the bands Petra and Second Chapter of Acts. Still, despite the wider exposure provided by record companies, Jesus rock could not break into Christian radio. Older audiences still preferred listening to preachers rather than up-tempo music.

By the 1980s, when many of the Jesus People had taken on the responsibilities of home-owning and child-rearing, the older genre of Jesus rock merged into CCM thanks to two different developments. The first was the recognition by main-stream recording industry executives that a market existed for gospel music, a designation that defied classification and could include country, folk, and rock and roll with religious lyrics. One entertainer who kept the recording industry interested in Christian music was Amy Grant, the first contemporary Christian artist to sell more than a million copies of a single album. Grant did so with *Age to Age* (1982), which stayed at the top of *Billboard* magazine's chart for "inspirational" music for more than 150 weeks. Her next album, *Straight Ahead* (1984), remained number one for a year, and Grant became the first gospel artist to register enough sales (one million copies) to achieve platinum status for one of her albums. Executives at A & M records now recognized the potential of the gospel market and acquired rights to Grant's album *Unguarded*, which achieved gold status (500,000 copies) only two months after release. Although Grant was unsuccessful in her attempt to leave behind her identity as an evangelical artist and cross over into the secular recording industry, her success in gospel music was nonetheless an indication that CCM had arrived as a significant partner in the entertainment industry. In 1999 it accounted for $450 million in sales.

The success of CCM, however, was not the doing of Amy Grant alone or the record executives who spotted her potential. In the years before 1990 the Christian music industry, though much more visible and profitable than it had been during the days of the Jesus People, lacked focus. Performers such as Grant could test the waters of the top-forty radio stations, but that strategy raised questions about the Christianness of the music. Or if CCM artists produced music only for evangelical youth, they still lacked access to Christian radio. There James Dobson may have recruited new listeners to his mix of down-home and professional advice about child-rearing, but the staple programs were evangelical pastors and evangelists such as Chuck Swindoll or Charles Stanley. In order to secure a larger religious audience, Christian performers needed to demonstrate clearly that their music was not simply a safe alternative for teens who might otherwise be tempted by Punk or Heavy Metal. Instead they had to show that this new music had explicitly religious ends.

Here the charismatic leaven of evangelical Protestantism came to the rescue. The charismatic movement had already emerged in the 1950s as an expressive and emotional strain of evangelical piety. It emphasized the immediate work of the Holy Spirit rather than correct doctrine or the authority of Scripture. Charismatics were indebted to Pentecostalism, which originated during the early twentieth century. In addition to stressing the need for the conversion experience, Pentecostals also taught that Christians could live at a higher plane of devotion after a second experience of the Holy Spirit, most characteristically demonstrated by speaking in tongues. When "slain" by the Spirit, these evangelicals would break into an unknown language. Throughout the first half of the twentieth century Pentecostalism remained a separate segment of evangelicalism and took institutional form in such denominations as the Assemblies of God and the Church of God. But after 1950 Pentecostal influence began to penetrate settings where speaking in tongues would have been out of place but not the more animated and flamboyant forms of Pentecostal worship that promised greater zeal and devotion. The charismatic movement was, in effect, the Pentecostal sensibility without the demand for tongues or for joining one of the historically Pentecostal denominations. It began to make itself evident in various parachurch organizations that attracted Christians from mainline, evangelical, and even Roman Catholic churches.

The greatest evidence of charismatic influence was the new form of worship that in the early 1970s began to surface throughout all sectors of American Christianity. Sometimes called Praise & Worship, charismatic worship appealed to believers who thought traditional Christian services were stuffy and cold. Interestingly, the Jesus People pioneered in these newer ways of worship. Chuck Smith was one minister who combined the new Christian music and worship. A California pastor in the Foursquare Gospel denomination, another of the churches in the Pentecostal orbit, Smith found denominational life in the 1960s to be stifling. Frustrated, he left his denomination in 1965 to found Calvary Chapel in Costa Mesa, California, and decided to focus his efforts on the hippies and surfers residing in the vicinity. He also included the music of the Jesus People in his worship services, to the point where he founded a record company, Maranatha Music, to record and distribute the new Christian music. Over time Smith's church blossomed into a network of churches, all adopting the name Calvary Chapel. A similar group of churches is the Vineyard Christian Fellowship, which dates from the 1970s and also uses charismatic styles of worship to reach young and sometimes disaffected evangelicals.

What was critical in the cases of both Calvary Chapel and the Vineyard was a form of worship that relies heavily on songs from the Christian music industry. The growth of these networks of churches, combined with their influence upon other Protestant congregations, proved to be a godsend for CCM. By 1990 Praise & Worship had become a popular option for churches that hoped to attract new members. Although it alienated older and more traditional evangelicals, it secured a wide hearing for Christian musicians. More important, it gave the new music the imprimatur of respectability it had lacked when it was simply an alternative and sanitized form of rock and roll for young people. CCM was not simply something to listen to in the car, it was also music to sing on Sunday morning in church.

Characteristic of this new form of evangelical worship is the presence of a "praise" band at the front of the church (though the buildings often look different from traditional church structures). The band usually consists of the very same ingredients that constituted Jesus rock—a set of drums, bass, and electric guitars, sometimes a synthesizer, and singers with hand-held microphones. The cultural icon of rock and roll has replaced the religious symbol of sacred choral music, the church choir. What typically transpires in these Praise & Worship services is an opening segment, sometimes lasting as long as thirty minutes, of praise songs, followed by prayer, another round of singing, and then the sermon to conclude the service. On one level the appeal is bound up with the musical idiom of contemporary music. Instead of experiencing something of a shock when going from popular music throughout the week to formal choral music on Sunday, now what evangelicals hear on the radio or in their homes is also something they may sing on Sunday morning. Yet the appeal of this kind of worship goes beyond familiarity. The earnestness of the music conveys a sense of intimacy that suggests being "in the grip of God." Since the eighteenth century, evangelicalism has thrived on its adherents' sense of an immediate encounter with God. Praise & Worship is simply the latest version of this typically evangelical outlook.

Yet if such experiences depend upon a particular form of music, one may well ask whether worshipers are sensing the movement of the Spirit or simply enjoying the music? The line between entertainment and devotion is particularly difficult to draw in the case of CCM and its outlet in contemporary evangelical worship. Praise & Worship aptly illustrates what has happened to evangelical ventures in the arena of popular culture, whether as producers or consumers. The experiential side of born-again Protestantism, from conversion to the trials of believers, turns out to provide highly entertaining material.

This is easier to see in the case of videos, film, radio theater, or novels, which rely upon a successful dramatic narrative. Here the story of a believer's encounter with sin and escape through conversion may function as either a tool for evangelism or wholesome entertainment for the converted. But even in a medium such as music, where beat, rhythm, tempo, and lyrics replace plot structure and character development, evangelicalism readily turns a form of entertainment into a crucial part of devotion. For although CCM began as a safer form of rock and roll for young evangelicals, when it found its way into Sunday morning worship this music became legitimate by demonstrating its capacity for edification.

In the end, CCM and Praise & Worship demonstrate evangelicalism's habit of expressing Christianity in vernacular and popular idioms. In some ways this is only a function of born-again Protestantism's discomfort with the churchly and official forms of Christianity that make the laity dependent on clergy. But the use of sophisticated technology or popular forms of entertainment to communicate a religious message also reflects evangelicalism's refusal to abide by the distinctions between the sacred and the secular. For evangelicals, all areas of life have a religious dimension. Consequently, distinguishing between the so-called worldly music of rock and roll and the devout music of churches is to deny the relevance of faith to all parts of human life. As the history of evangelical reactions to and participation in American popular culture also shows, however, sometimes the distinctions that born-again Protestants oppose are also crucial to determining whether a particular cultural expression is in fact religious. Without that kind of distinction, evangelicalism's instinct for finding non-traditional forms of devotion may send the inconsistent message that a song, novel, or movie is religious when it really is not.

The difficulty of determining where religion ends and entertainment begins was graphically illustrated in 1997 with the release of Amy Grant's CD *Behind the Eyes* (1997). This was another of the performer's efforts to cross over from the CCM audience to the "secular" market. The *Rolling Stone* of CCM, *Contemporary Christian Music* magazine, judged the CD to be "definitely faith-revealing." But a letter to the editor shot back, "A Christian album should be clear on the person of Christ, and these lyrics are not." Responses that read like this one to Grant's disk prompted a warning to radio stations: "As far as the lyrical content is concerned, there's no evangelical bent, no mention of God. If the music you play has to have either of these two elements, you might not want to play it." Evangelical critics of Grant believed their judgments were valid, especially when only two years later she divorced her husband, an apparent indication that her evangelical commitment had not only flagged but had led to a flagrant violation of biblical teaching.

The Grant episode illustrates more than the risk that CCM artists run in trying to move outside the evangelical fold into the mainstream entertainment industry. It also reflects more broadly the difficulty that late-twentieth-century evangelicals faced when they left the subculture of their parents and grandparents to participate in the wider culture. Entering public policy debates and electoral politics was dangerous. Born-again Protestants had to take their beliefs and convictions from spheres where Scripture and expectations for conversion were natural into wider settings where such convictions were not only unique but contested. The experience of evangelicals in the realm of entertainment offers another version of the same lesson. When the faith of believers goes from private settings where the participants share the same religious convictions to public ones where audiences are religiously mixed, either the faith or the audience has to give. Either evangelicals are forced to smooth the edges that non-evangelicals might find rough, or they face playing before smaller crowds.

In some ways this is a dilemma unique to evangelicals because of the public impulse in their faith. An inherent desire for new converts drives born-again Protestants to make their faith known to nonbelievers. On the other hand, the idea that religion affects all areas of life prompts evangelicals to make faith evident and explicit in any number of settings, from politics to rock and roll. And evangelicals are well versed in using any and all forms of cultural expression to advance their religion. In other versions of Christianity, adherents are often more content to relegate religious devotion to private spheres of church and family life, or to parochial schooling, settings that are clearly set off from public ones. Because evangelicalism has historically resisted this form of bifurcation, every generation of born-again Protestants faces the dilemma of how best to make Christianity accessible to non-Christians without watering down the message or offending the listener.

The root of this problem is deeper than the contemporary scene which finds evangelicals well-educated, prosperous, and rubbing shoulders with all sorts of Americans in any number of settings. Even during the first half of the twentieth century, when evangelicals were much more suspicious of "worldliness" and so cut themselves off from American society, their understanding of Christianity's divine and supernatural character prevented them from relating their faith to the world in a comfortable manner. The discrepancy between things divine and things human was so wide because of the belief that involvement in affairs outside the church—politics, music, literature, ideas—could proceed only if such affairs had religious significance. If they did not, they were at best a waste of time or at worst sinful. From 1920 to 1960 evangelicals generally viewed these worldly affairs as something in which Christians should not participate. From 1960 to 2000 this estimate changed. But the logic beneath either withdrawal or participation was the same. For an activity to be worthy of an evangelical's attention, it needed to advance Christianity. Through their engagement with the world outside their parents' and grandparents' subculture, the most recent generation of evangelicals has begun to experience the inconsistencies in this logic. They are learning that the politics and culture of the United States are not so readily turned to Christian ends.

7

Evangelical Misunderstandings

EVANGELICALISM is one of the more difficult religions in the United States to understand. Part of the problem is the movement's lack of boundaries or formal status. No single denomination claims to be the Evangelical Church of America. If such an entity did exist, researchers and students of religion in the United States could look at the denomination's founding documents, history, publications, hymnal, church government, and creed to determine what it means to be evangelical, in the same way that one may in the case of Roman Catholicism, Episcopalianism, or Methodism. In other words, evangelicalism is a movement, not a church, and it has thrived outside the formal channels of denominational assemblies and agencies. Evangelicalism is therefore quintessentially a parachurch form of Christianity, leaving the formal matters of church life to the bureaucrats and clergy while winning the hearts, minds, and pocketbooks of those sitting in the pews.

But born-again Protestantism is not simply hard to decipher because it ranges beyond traditional religious structures. It also sends conflicting messages to nonevangelicals in the United States (and for that matter around the world) that raise questions which evangelicals themselves are hard pressed to answer. On the one hand, evangelical Protestants have over the last two decades of the twentieth century been strenuously involved in American electoral politics. However successful they have been, evangelicals have established a reputation as adamantly conservative. After all, they comprise the religious *right*. On moral issues they seek to reflect biblical ethics in the nation's laws; on domestic and international issues evangelicals vote overwhelmingly for candidates who advocate free markets and a strong national defense. On the other hand, evangelicals have become one of the largest markets in the United States' already crowded entertainment industry. Christian Contemporary Music alone accounts for $747 million in annual sales, a figure which means that seven evangelical CDs are sold for every ten country music disks. What makes evangelical music hard to figure, however, is that the most popular musicians are those who sing and write religious words to rock and roll, a form of music not well known for promoting the family values that evangelical politicians and activists trumpet. In sum, evangelicals appear to be the most traditional of Americans and at the same time they give evidence of being the most up to date.

The most common way of interpreting American evangelicalism is to see it as the conservative wing of Protestantism. According to this perspective, Protestantism in the United States is divided between a liberal party and a conservative one; the mainline churches that are members of the ecumenical National Council of Churches are liberal Protestants, and evangelicals are the conservative ones. As such, evangelicalism stands for those essential parts of Christianity to which American Protestantism adhered before the fundamentalist controversy of the 1920s. The necessity of being born again, the divine and infallible nature of the Bible, and the importance of such doctrines as the virgin birth of Christ, the atonement and resurrection—these are teachings the mainline churches softened during the early decades of the twentieth century, and evangelicalism has kept them alive. This helps explain evangelicalism's reputation as an essentially conservative faith. It is, according to many scholars, nothing less than the old-time religion.

Understanding evangelicalism as fundamentally conservative appears to make sense of the religious right, but not Christian rock and roll. If born-again Protestants represent an older style of Christian faith, and if conservative politicians seek to preserve the kinds of ideals that contributed to the United States' emergence as a superpower, one can understand, even predict, evangelicalism's support for conservative politicians. But again, the image of evangelicalism becomes fuzzy once the Christian entertainment industry is added to the picture. Although evangelical music, for instance, offers a safe alternative for teens whose parents want a form of rock and roll that will not glamorize sex and drugs, it is hardly preserving sacred music from the past. As conservatives—religiously, politically, and culturally—evangelicals might naturally prefer Bach and Beethoven to DC Talk or Amy Grant. Yet in the realm of popular culture evangelicals are among the most sensitive to the latest trends. One possible explanation is the evangelistic drive that prompts born-again Protestants to find new ways of exposing unbelievers to Christianity, with contemporary music providing the most recent alternative. In effect, evangelicals rock in order to proclaim the gospel. Still, the incongruity between a timeless message and a perpetually novel cultural idiom is difficult to harmonize.

A better way of understanding evangelicals may be to abandon the categories of conservative and liberal and recognize that this form of Protestantism originated well before the polarizations of the twentieth century. Thus to call evangelicalism conservative is anachronistic. It also obscures the dynamic of born-again Protestant devotion that motivates both the politics of the religious right and the ingenuity of Christian Contemporary Music's performers and entrepreneurs.

Here it is important to see that evangelical Protestantism is fundamentally a form of pietism. Pietism is a word steeped in theological and historical nuance, but the primary emphasis of this version of Protestantism is the cultivation of godly zeal and behavior through personal practices of devotion. Another way of putting this is to say that pietism demands and looks for evidence of genuine religion in affairs not typically considered sacred or religious. Pietists fear a kind of faith where adherents simply go through the motions of church attendance and deference to the ministry of church officers. Church practices may too easily be faked. Consequently the true convert needs to show his or her zeal outside the confines of the church. A dramatic experience of divine presence, such as a conversion, is one way to demonstrate a genuine faith. But for pietists, conversion is just the start and is inconsequential if not accompanied by strenuous and visible morality. For this reason pietists not only stress the conversion experience but also an earnest moral life that sets a believer apart from the rest of society. Understanding evangelicalism as a version of pietism, then, helps to make sense both of Jesus rock and the religious right. CCM demonstrates the genius of articulating Christianity in ways different from those traditionally used by churches, while the politics of the religious right reflects pietism's demand for holy living.

Another feature of pietism that helps account for some of the anomalies of contemporary evangelicalism is a refusal to relegate religion to a particular sphere of life. Although other expressions of Christianity, both Protestant and Roman Catholic, have clearly demonstrated the capacity to influence social and cultural endeavors well beyond the scope of the church, they also adhere to teachings that distinguish things religious from more secular or public affairs. In its official character the church has a particular set of responsibilities, sacred ones, that are distinct from authorities or institutions established to oversee other arenas, from politics to education. This is a distinction, however, that pietists resist. The objection is that such segmentation of religion into a churchly realm, and the other areas of life into a secular or public arena, ends up divorcing religion from those other enterprises and therefore denies the importance of faith for all of life. As spiritual descendants of pietism, evangelicals have well exhibited this opposition to the compartmentalization of religion. Born-again Protestants regularly assert that faith is not only relevant but of vital importance to every walk of life because God is the creator and sustainer of every aspect of creation. To relegate religion to one day of the week and to the activities of the church is simply to deny divine sovereignty over human affairs on all the other days of the week.

The irony of evangelicalism's history in the United States is that this form of Protestantism has flourished in a nation founded on a secular platform. To be sure, the founders relied upon generically Christian teachings in their understanding of politics and the good society, and a few of the individual states continued to support established churches through tax revenues. Even so, the Constitution clearly set down the principle that faith would not be a qualification for holding federal office; the affairs of the United States government would have to be conducted without input from churches, synagogues, mosques, or temples. Yet, despite the secular design of American statecraft, evangelicalism became the dominant religious expression in the United States. This was partly the result of evangelical tenacity in seeking new converts and sending out evangelists as the new nation expanded, along with the host of voluntary benevolent enterprises that born-again Protestants sponsored. It also owed to the cultural homogeneity of the American population. Anglo-American Protestants were most numerous and held positions of power. No wonder their faith provided a moral consensus for the new nation.

Just as important to evangelical prominence, though, was the pietist notion that genuine religion extended beyond church activities to all realms of life. This impulse prompted evangelicals to become involved in a variety of social and cultural affairs that if conducted under the sponsorship of the church would have raised questions about the establishment of religion. But because born-again Protestantism does not depend on the formalities of church life, evangelicals could take their faith into various secular affairs without apparently violating the separation between church and state. Although that wall of separation may have made clergy who became active in public life appear suspect, it posed few barriers to a form of Protestantism that encouraged the laity to practice their faith in every arena of life. In other words, pietism circumvented distinctions between church and state, or between the religious and the secular. It not only asserted that all of life was religious but also avoided confinement in official structures, like those of the church, which American politics clearly restrained.

Although pietism provided evangelicals with a rationale that allowed faith to seep into every human arena, it also obscured the profoundly secular character of the nation they so actively supported. Again, the cultural homogeneity of the United States throughout the nineteenth century prevented evangelicals from seeing the inconsistency of their aspirations for a publicly relevant religion in the United States. As long as most Americans were evangelical Protestants—a statistic that a large influx of immigrants between 1870 and 1910 began to modify—the presence of religion in matters outside the church was not obviously a problem. But evangelical blindness to the dilemmas posed by secularization also stemmed from born-again faith itself. By blurring the distinction between things religious and things secular, evangelicals were unprepared for the kinds of restrictions upon religion that would finally manifest themselves in the twentieth century, when public officials tried to accommodate the actual diversity of faiths in the United States. The logic implicit in the separation of church and state was to make religion private, thereby creating a space for public life free from religious dispute. This logic was unclear during the nineteenth century as evangelicals participated freely in public life on the basis of their convictions and baptized the American experiment as fundamentally Christian. Once the need for religious neutrality became apparent, evangelicals were ill prepared because of their conviction that no sphere of life is religiously neutral.

The first signs of evangelical unpreparedness for a secular America came during the 1920s when the oldest Protestant denominations divided between fundamentalists and liberals. Evangelicals began to lose status partly owing to their defense of the Bible's divine character. Their devotion to Scripture prevented them from adapting to significant changes in American learning and public policy that liberal Protestants were trying to accommodate. As such, evangelicals became identified as uneducated and backward, and their marginalization from America's leading institutions of education prompted born-again Protestants to retreat into their own religious subculture. In their own world of prophecy conferences, Bible institutes, evangelical magazines, Christian radio programs, and foreign missions, born-again Protestants thrived and established an identity as a people set apart from a godless society. They saw their purpose as saving as many souls as possible before the impending judgment. Ironically, the larger society was not so godless as to have marginalized all forms of faith. Consequently, even as evangelicals sequestered themselves in their own subculture, their nemesis, the mainline Protestant denominations, maintained the vestiges of Christian civilization in the United States, thus affording born-again Protestants the luxury of cultural and social isolation in a society where Protestant mores received implicit support.

But once even the trappings of Christian society began to wear away during the 1960s, evangelicals gained a sense of what a more overtly secular society looked like. In one sense the kinds of changes that occurred during that tumultuous decade caused many public officials to see that Protestantism had historically enjoyed a privileged status in the United States and that government and other public institutions had to strive to be neutral or evenhanded in the treatment of all faiths. But a number of the protest movements of the 1960s also included outright hostility to the religion of Protestants, not only because this faith had been unfairly privileged but because of its apparently repressive ethic.

At this point evangelical perceptions that America was drifting from its religious roots gained a measure of accuracy. Evangelicals' response was to leave the spiritually nurturing confines of their religious subculture and contend for the necessity of religion in public life. The most visible aspect of this movement was the religious right. But evangelicals gained attention in other arenas as well, such as popular culture and higher education. The net effect was the growing prominence of a faith once discredited as backward and marginal in a society that was rapidly becoming secular. The coincidence of evangelicalism's reawakening and the secularization of American society left many journalists and academics scratching their heads. How was it that a traditional faith could flourish in a modern democratic and highly industrialized society? Evangelicals were, in effect, beating all the odds and proving that secularization did not necessarily involve the death of religion.

Nevertheless, although evangelicalism offered an inspiring story of an underdog faith prevailing over enormous obstacles, born-again Protestants had trouble resolving the tension between religion and secularity. Evangelicals may have been admirable for their resilience and perseverance, but they have had trouble convincing some Americans, first, that religion should significantly inform public and cultural life, and, second, how this influence should manifest itself. The reason for this difficulty is that evangelicals have primarily viewed secular society as a problem in need of a religious solution. For them the key to America's prosperity and freedom in the past, present, and future is faith, and the elimination of religion from public life necessarily means decay and immorality. Yet what evangelicals have had trouble understanding is that the emergence of secularism in the United States since the 1960s was not simply the result of animosity to faith. To be sure, some Americans have welcomed a diminished role for religion in the nation's culture because they view faith as a form of superstition and oppression. But secularization also occurred because religion no longer provided the social purpose and cultural cohesion it once had (whether it should have or not). In fact, Protestantism looked very divisive in the context of the 1960s debates over race, gender, and Vietnam. One way to resolve the difficulty was to sequester religion to the private sphere and establish a public realm that was as religiously neutral as possible.

The irony of this resolution to American Protestantism's former dominance is that at the very same time many American leaders recognized the wisdom of separating religion from public life, evangelicals were reemerging from their self-imposed isolation to reassert the importance of religion to *all* walks of life. Indeed, evangelicals' opposition to secularization includes more than simply the sense that to threaten the place of Christianity in the United States is to condemn the nation to wreck and ruin. It also involves the pietist premise that faith, to be genuine, needs to be evident in all realms. Evangelicalism, accordingly, is necessarily uncomfortable with any effort to confine religion to its own sphere. Born-again Protestants not only believe that this is impossible because faith, if genuine, is necessarily pervasive. They also regard the effort to segregate faith, to make it private, as an affront to their own religion because evangelicalism teaches precisely the reverse. The result is an inherent antagonism between evangelicalism and secularization. Secular society assumes a distinction between the public sectors of government, business, and education, for instance, and the private ones of family, churches, and voluntary associations. Because of their belief that faith is all pervasive, evangelicals refuse to accept an arrangement where public realms that involve Christians and non-Christians are religiously neutral and private realms that include believers only are reserved for religion.

The advantage of this refusal to quarantine religion for evangelicals is evident in their innovative approaches to attract new converts. The most recent example of evangelical creativity is the megachurch phenomenon, a form of congregational life that is self-consciously designed to make non-Christians feel at home in church. An article in the August 1996 issue of the *Atlantic Monthly* aptly described this latest endeavor by evangelicals to remove the mystery surrounding religion and make it user-friendly: "No spires. No crosses. No robes. No clerical collars. No hard pews. No kneelers. No biblical gobbledygook. No prayerly rote. No fire, no brimstone. No pipe organs. No dreary eighteenth-century hymns. No forced solemnity. No Sunday finery. No collection plates." Many evangelicals are abandoning all these habits of Protestant church life, the article explained, to clear the way for "new, contemporary forms of worship and belonging."

What is immediately striking about these new church forms is size. Many of the congregations count more than ten thousand people attending services each week, hence the name "megachurch." In addition to size, these churches defy expectations by meeting in structures that have more of the feel of corporate offices than a church building. Some of the new facilities even include food courts, complete with "a cappuccino cart . . . dispensing the secular sacrament." But aside from the size of the crowds and buildings (and parking lots) to accommodate them, the most notable aspect of this new line of evangelical outreach is worship. The *Atlantic* article reported that the megachurch draws people "by being relentlessly creative about developing forms of worship—most symbolically and specifically, music—that are contemporary, accessible, 'authentic.'" Services feature praise bands, skits, and lots of electronic equipment. In fact, music turns out to be the defining element of these new evangelical congregations. "Whether a church uses contemporary music or not defines which kind of people it wants. When it uses contemporary music, it's saying it wants unchurched people—particularly those of child-bearing and child-rearing age." As one CCM executive told the *Atlantic*'s writer, "We better think about our sound and how we are reaching our community, or we will be the Amish of the twenty-first century."

Of course, the use of religious forms in synch with contemporary culture has characterized evangelicalism since its origins in the eighteenth century. Its leaders have had a remarkable capacity for sensing novel cultural developments and turning them to Christianity's advantage. In this sense the megachurch phenomenon is really as old as George Whitefield, one of the first evangelicals to use new forms of music, new media and technology, and new economic structures in the work of making new Christians.

What the rise of megachurches also illustrates is the foundation upon which evangelicalism so readily adapts to new social and cultural realities. By blurring the line between religion and other forms of human endeavor and interaction, evangelicals have practically no compunction about taking something that has nothing to do with sacred or divine matters, and may even appear to be hostile to faith, and turning it into a spiritual asset. Here the rationale is not simply the desire to make new converts which accounts in part for differences between evangelical innovations and other Protestants' traditionalism. The ability to employ apparently secular phenomena for religious ends rests ultimately on evangelicalism's rejection of the dichotomy between the sacred and the secular. If every part of a Christian's life has the same degree of religious significance, expressions of faith may take as many forms as humanly possible. For this reason, evangelicals in the United States have always outstripped other Protestants in accomplishing what scholars who study missions call making faith "culturally indigenous." Except when it exhibits explicit forms of sinful behavior, the surrounding culture poses no barrier to evangelicals looking for ways to express their faith. This explains why some have concluded that evangelicalism is a quintessentially American religion.

As much as this denial of the distinction between the public and the private aids the proselytizing efforts of born-again Protestants, it turns out to be a serious handicap politically. This is one realm of American life where religion is genuinely divisive, partly because of laws that prohibit the establishment of religion and partly owing to the sheer diversity of faiths in the United States. Unlike the positive coverage that evangelicalism receives for its innovations in making religion accessible to large numbers of people, many of the same journalists point to born-again Protestantism's tin ear for appreciating the music of the public arena.

A good illustration of reports that found evangelicals incredibly clumsy (or worse) in the political process were those that followed the scandal surrounding president Bill Clinton's relationship with White House intern Monica Lewinsky. In a piece for the *New York Times Magazine*, Andrew Sullivan, former editor of *The New Republic*, asserted that the Clinton-Lewinsky affair had revealed the bankruptcy of the Republican party and political conservatism. "The conservative movement," he wrote, "has lost sight of the principle of government restraint and of the boundary between public and private, the very things that made it a successful political force in America." Whether or not that distinction between the public and private was actually responsible for conservatism's success is debatable. But Sullivan added that part of the reason for conservatives' failure was the growing prominence of evangelical Protestants in the Republican party. "The issues that are driving the Republican base . . . have little to do with economics or politics or national security." Instead they were all moral questions: "infidelity and honesty, abortion, family cohesion and homosexual legitimacy." These were precisely the issues that had motivated evangelicals since the founding of the Moral Majority. But by the time of the Clinton-Lewinsky scandal, Sullivan complained, they had turned political conservatives into "scolds." Although he did not mention that the independent counsel overseeing the government's investigation, Kenneth W. Starr, was an evangelical, Sullivan did not need to. Readers who had been following the scandal knew of Starr's evangelical identity, and his role in the investigation only added to the perception that born-again Protestants were self-righteous tattletales.

Sullivan's successor at *The New Republic*, Peter Beinart, described the influence of evangelicals on American politics a year or so later when he noted an irony on which few journalists had commented. That irony involved the similarities between the religious right and their political antagonists, the feminists. Beinart wrote:

> As recently as the 1960s, women and evangelicals played virtually no role in public policy. Feminism and the Christ-

ian right responded to this powerlessness in similar ways—
by defining politics as something that occurred not in the
halls of government but in the consciousness of individuals
and in their conduct at home. Public policy was not a separate moral space with its own rules, but a reflection of the
way people lived their lives. In this way, the two movements politicized their followers and overcame their mar-
ginality. Today, both are powerful players in government.
But their ideologies of government have not changed. They
still assert that public policy is a mere representation of the
personal lives of those who make it. And that idea, let loose
in Washington, has left American politics in shambles.

Aside from observing the strange coincidence of evangelicals
following in the footsteps of the women's movement and turning the personal into the political, Beinart's point reflected the
perspective of many liberals who faulted evangelicals for
gumming up the political machinery with moral matters that
were private and personal. But what made the observation
particularly poignant was that Beinart blamed evangelicals for
fusing the public and the private. These Christians, he concluded, pursued public policy with the expectation that government should be "a reflection of the soul."

Conflicting perceptions of evangelical religion (such as
megachurches) and evangelical politics (such as the religious
right) illustrate the difficulty of making sense of born-again
Protestantism. On the one hand, evangelicals clearly offer a
version of Christianity that is accessible to people intimidated
by the somber and mysterious ways of traditional churches.
Here the blurring of lines between things religious and things
common allows born-again Protestants to be innovative, flexi-
ble, and even fun. On the other hand, when it comes to public
life the image of evangelicals changes dramatically. To many
non-Christians, the insistence that political realities must conform to privately held religious ideals looks puritanical, self-

righteous, and narrow. In other words, evangelicals seem to be inherently inconsistent, striking a pose at once adaptable and rigid, progressive and conservative, modern and old-fashioned, at ease and at odds with American ideals. The result of these apparent anomalies is a religion that on Sunday is comfortable with the church looking like the world (such as CCM) and throughout the rest of the week insists that the world look like the church (as in family values).

If the two faces of evangelicalism stem from the movement's pietistic refusal to divorce religion from other facets of human endeavor, its pietistic outlook also accounts for evangelicalism's misunderstanding of secular society. In a nutshell, evangelicals are inherently uncomfortable with the diminished role for faith under secularization. According to the sociologist Steve Bruce, the smaller role for faith in modern society is the result of a variety of large social forces that emerged as early as the sixteenth century. But the contemporary outworking of these trends is clear. Bruce writes:

> Our societies permit (and in some places even encourage) the maintenance of distinctive religious world-views and thus encourage socio-moral contests, but they also create a structure (the division of the life world into public and private spheres) and a culture (universalism and tolerance) which of necessity restrain such contests and require that they be fought on general universalistic ethical and public-policy principles. In modern democratic culturally plural societies, no socio-moral interest group can plausibly promote its case on the grounds that "the Bible (or the Koran or the Book of Mormon) says so." Instead it must argue that equity or reason or the public good says so.

Richard John Neuhaus, editor of the journal *First Things* and a thoughtful critic of the anti-religious bias in contemporary American public policy, also thinks evangelicals misunderstand the way faith relates to public life in a secular society such as the United States. The religious right, he warns,

> wants to enter the political arena making claims on the basis of private truths. The integrity of politics itself requires that such a proposal be resisted. Public decisions must be made by arguments that are public in character. . . . Fundamentalist morality, which is derived from beliefs that cannot be submitted to examination by public reason, is essentially a private morality. If enough people who share that morality are mobilized, it can score victories in the public arena. But every such victory is a setback in the search for a public ethic.

A recent book by Christian Smith, the same University of North Carolina sociologist discussed in the introduction, questions these assessments by Bruce and Neuhaus. In a sequel study, *Christian America? What Evangelicals Really Want*, Smith uses extensive phone interviews with ordinary born-again Protestants to reveal much more nuance, tolerance, and ambiguity than evangelicals are usually given credit for. The word "ordinary" is key to Smith's analysis, because he holds that the average evangelical sees secular society differently from such born-again leaders as James Dobson, Pat Robertson, or Jerry Falwell. This is an interesting point with some merit, though it does not take into account that most of the ordinary people Smith interviewed are the same ones who make Dobson's, Robertson's, and Falwell's broadcasts into multimillion-dollar enterprises.

Even so, the notion of "Christian America," according to Smith, is not actually the threat that non-Christian observers perceive it to be. He identifies six different strands that comprise the Christian America evangelicals desire. The first is a sense that the United States was founded to protect religious liberty. The second is that Christians constitute a majority of Americans who "put their beliefs and morals into practice . . .

faithfully." The third idea concerns the character of laws in the United States, which evangelicals believe should be based upon Christian principles. Fourth, when referring to the United States as a Christian nation, evangelicals often appeal to the example of the Founding Fathers who prayed to God and tried to follow divine will in creating a new nation. A fifth way in which evangelicals speak of the United States as Christian involves the Christian values and principles that have informed public life throughout much of the nation's history. Finally, evangelicals interviewed by Smith conceive of Christian America as a place where public displays of religious symbols during religious holidays are an acceptable and normal practice. These responses lead to the conclusion that the evangelical idea of Christian America does not involve an establishment of religion or coercive legislation. "Most evangelicals in fact do not long with obsessive nostalgia for a Christian past that they hope to restore," Smith writes. "They have no intention of rolling back America's cultural and religious pluralism through the reestablishment of Christianity."

As reassuring as this assessment may be, the fine print in this same book reveals a very different impression, one that confirms the point that evangelicals do not know what to do in an increasingly secularized society where Protestantism was once dominant. In an appendix to his book, Smith compares evangelicals to other Americans, and sometimes the results indeed suggest, as the author thinks they do, that born-again Protestant attitudes toward public displays of immorality and the anti-religious bias of the media differ little from those of their nonevangelical neighbors. For instance, 92 percent of evangelicals and 80 percent of all other Americans say that "moral decay" is the "main cause" of the United States' problems. Also, about the same number of evangelicals and nonevangelicals, approximately one-quarter, support the idea of declaring the United States a Christian nation through a constitutional amendment. On other measures, however, evangelicals show themselves to be much more concerned than other Americans about irreligion and secular values. Two-thirds of evangelicals, compared with one-third of Americans, believe that public morality should be based upon an "absolute, unchanging standard." At the same time, twice as many evangelicals (two-thirds) as nonevangelicals (one-third) regard religion as a "publicly relevant matter," not to be excluded from public policy debates. The net result of this evidence leads Smith to conclude that "ordinary conservative Protestants do tend to be significantly more supportive of some of the claims of the Christian Right than other Americans—often 20 to 40 percentage points more so." If this observation does not contradict Smith's main point about the tolerance and flexibility of ordinary evangelicals, it certainly lends credence to the idea that born-again Protestants are uncomfortable with a society where Christianity is not the norm.

One of the ways Smith attempts to skirt the apparent inconsistency of his findings is to distinguish between personal and legal forms of evangelical influence. In countless interviews, evangelicals told researchers that politics is not the best way to exert a religious presence in America. The better tactic, they said, is through one-on-one testimonials or by living exemplary lives. According to one woman from Michigan:

> We can turn back to a Christian heritage by not supporting some of these TV programs—shutting off the TV, for one thing. Violence, murder, love stories, soap operas. Watching how we present ourselves. Saying no to drugs and alcohol. Not supporting the movie industry that is showing lots of junk. Trying to outdo one another in sharing with one another, really being a neighbor to someone.

A man from Pennsylvania expressed the ideal form of evangelical involvement this way:

If you believe the scriptures, then a gay lifestyle is wrong. But that doesn't mean we are to be out there eradicating them. We are to try to persuade them that this is not God's design. They have always existed and will continue to. Our job is to be patient, to be concerned, and to let them know our viewpoint.

On the basis of responses like these, Smith concludes that "most ordinary evangelicals" hold that through personal relationships and by sharing the truth of Christianity with non-believers, "the unbelieving world will see the truth and voluntarily respond with a changed heart."

This is precisely the point that Hugh Hewitt makes in his 1998 book, *The Embarrassed Believer: Reviving Christian Witness in an Age of Unbelief.* An assistant counsel in the Reagan administration, the producer of the PBS series *Searching for God in America*, and the host of a daily syndicated radio talk show, Hewitt believes that the gravest problem confronting evangelicals is their shyness, if not embarrassment, in sharing Christianity with other Americans. Although Smith may be more optimistic about the possibility of evangelicals' personal influence, Hewitt wrote his book in part because of evangelical timidity. "The church in the United States," Hewitt asserts, "cannot genuinely be renewed and serve as a vehicle for revival unless its members witness with the boldness that Paul urged on Timothy"—"Do not be ashamed then of testifying to our Lord." Hewitt's book is an impassioned plea for Christian renewal, not a dispassionate study of sociological data, and his call for confident and assertive evangelicals makes Smith's defense of born-again Protestants look timid by comparison. Yet at bottom Smith and Hewitt agree that the key to evangelical influence is the capacity of individual evangelicals to bear witness to the truth of their beliefs.

Even so, personal example and conversation, as opposed to

political strategy, have their limits if Hewitt's book is any indication. For one of the points that emerges in *The Embarrassed Believer* is that the truth of evangelical Christianity is a means toward national greatness and public morality, not an end in itself. In one section of the book Hewitt discusses recent work by public intellectuals, such as the historian Gertrude Himmelfarb and the legal scholar Stephen Carter, that laments the breakdown of commonly recognized moral standards. Although Hewitt compliments these authors for their diagnosis, he criticizes them for not recognizing the truth of Christianity as the solution. These authors, Hewitt argues, write books that "condemn a moral relativism they themselves are embracing" by relegating faith to the private and personal sphere. Hewitt does not believe, however, that affirming Christianity as the only way of salvation will pose a threat to Americans. At one point he suggests that the "destruction of confident Christianity" is directly related to a collapse in "the quality of life" in America. To illustrate the point, Hewitt writes: "Our culture is pulverizing youth—destroying their bodies and their souls. Our culture is savaging families, and its endless, ceaseless eroticism is attacking the dignity of women on a new, uninterrupted basis. The music is vile, and most of the films plumb evil's depths rather than goodness's heights." The solution, then, to the United States moral wasteland is for believers to say that Christianity is true and it works.

Although Hewitt asserts the importance of personal evangelism and avoids political platforms, his reference is almost entirely public or social. Unlike the Amish, for example, who use religious liberty to carve out their own subculture, evangelicals are not content with a private space for their religion. The example of the Amish may be too extreme, but the case of Roman Catholicism in the United States works just as well. Many Catholics may distinguish the affairs of the church from those of civil society, and may enter the public realm mainly to

protect the well-being of church members or the work of
the church, but evangelicals do not differentiate between the
public and the private. Consequently when they enter the civil
realm they invariably do so with intentions of Christianizing
everything they do. This is why even the distinction between
evangelicals as a political interest group and evangelicals as ordinary believers seeking to influence through personal example breaks down. Inherent in evangelicalism is the idea that
religion applies to all of life. And the history of evangelicals in
America testifies to the former importance of Protestantism in
the life of the nation. For evangelicals to be content simply
with a piece but not the whole of American life is to betray the
claims of evangelical religion and ignore the lessons of American history.

At the end of *Christian America*, Smith helpfully points out
that most assessments of evangelicals in the United States portray born-again Protestants as either angels or demons. This
mythology, he adds, distorts evangelicalism rather than yielding greater understanding. To conclude that evangelicals misunderstand the nature of secular society and their role in it, as
this book does, could look like another example of mytholo-
gizing evangelicalism, this time on the demonic side. Yet the
point of noting evangelicalism's uneasiness in secular America
is not to vilify but actually to increase our understanding of
born-again Protestants' apparent awkwardness in modern society. Evangelicalism does not give its adherents the tools to
adapt to a secular United States, because this faith cannot separate religious concerns from public ones. At the same time
the history of American evangelicalism teaches its heirs that
born-again Protestants possess a noble history of social and
cultural influence. Evangelicalism tempts born-again Protestants to think, as Hugh Hewitt apparently does, that Americans will ultimately be better off with the faith of evangelicals.
It also causes nonevangelicals, like Larry and Phil, the sales-

men in *The Big Kahuna* mentioned at the beginning of this book, to view Bob, their unembarrassed evangelical colleague, with bewilderment and caution.

In the end, understanding evangelical misreadings of secular society in the United States may not prevent evangelicals like Bob from witnessing to the big kahuna on company time, or nonevangelicals like Larry from wrestling Bob to the floor. But it does identify one source of the friction.

A Note on Sources

ALTHOUGH EVANGELICALISM remains one of the most difficult expressions of Christianity to define, since 1980 it has also attracted considerable attention from American religious historians. What Martin E. Marty lamented in 1982 as "the paucity of good research" on born-again Protestantism is no longer the case. One index to this change is the publication of three reference works dedicated exclusively to evangelical Protestantism: *Twentieth-Century Evangelicalism: A Guide to the Sources*, edited by Edith L. Blumhofer and Joel A. Carpenter (New York, 1990); *American Evangelicalism: An Annotated Bibliography*, edited by Norris A. Magnuson (West Cornwall, Conn., 1990); and *American Evangelicalism II: First Bibliographical Supplement, 1990–1996*, edited by Norris A. Magnuson (West Cornwall, Conn., 1997). These bibliographies not only demonstrate the growth of scholarly interest in evangelicalism but are valuable reference works for further study.

General introductions to evangelicalism are available from a number of well-informed scholars. Mark A. Noll, *American Evangelical Christianity: An Introduction* (Oxford, England, 2001), and David Bebbington, *Evangelicalism in Modern Britain: A History from the 1730s to the 1980s* (London, 1989), though examining born-again Protestantism on different sides of the Atlantic, yield important insights into the inner workings of evangelical conviction while showing how such zeal plays out in different circumstances. Another highly useful historical introduction is Robert H. Krapohl and Charles H. Lippy, *The Evangelicals: A Historical, Thematic, and Biographical Guide* (Westport, Conn., 1999). A number of valuable collections of essays also provide details on specific episodes or movements in American evangelical history, and taken collectively offer a reliable overview of the movement.

Here *The Evangelical Tradition in America*, edited by Leonard I.
Sweet (Macon, Ga., 1984); *Evangelicalism: Comparative Studies of
Popular Protestantism in North America, The British Isles, and Be-
yond, 1700–1900*, edited by Mark A. Noll, David W. Bebbington,
and George A. Rawlyk (New York, 1994); and *The Variety of
American Evangelicalism*, edited by Donald W. Dayton and
Robert K. Johnston (Knoxville, Tenn., 1991) are well worth in-
vestigation. Randall Balmer, *Encyclopedia of Evangelicalism*
(Louisville, 2002), is also useful in providing brief, accessible articles on born-again individuals, institutions, and beliefs.

Historians locate the origins of evangelicalism as a distinct
form of Protestant Christianity in the revivals of the eighteenth
century, the so-called First Great Awakening. But the religious
and moral zeal that transformed colonial Protestantism also
had deeper roots in European pietism and English Puritanism.
Works that examine the pietist awakenings among European
Protestants include W. R. Ward, *The Protestant Evangelical
Awakening* (New York, 1992), and F. Ernest Stoeffler, *The Rise of
Evangelical Pietism* (Leiden, 1971). For the way pietism worked
its way into colonial American Protestantism, see F. Ernest Stoeffler, *Continental Pietism and Early American Christianity* (Grand
Rapids, 1976), and Randall H. Balmer, *A Perfect Babel of Confu-
sion: Dutch Religion and English Culture in the Middle Colonies*
(New York, 1989). The Puritan contribution to evangelical con-
ceptions of conversion can be gleaned from Alan Simpson, *Puritanism in Old and New England* (Chicago, 1955); Charles Lloyd
Cohen, *God's Caress: The Psychology of Puritan Religious Experience* (New York, 1986); Harold P. Simonson, *Jonathan Edwards:
Theologian of the Heart* (Grand Rapids, 1974); and Charles E.
Hambrick-Stowe, *The Practice of Piety: Puritan Devotional Discipline in Seventeenth-century New England* (Chapel Hill, 1982).
Jonathan Edwards's contribution to the formation of evangelicalism was considerable. The best source on the formulation of his
ideas about the priority of heart religion, which includes a helpful orientation on the relationship between American revivalism
and its Protestant antecedents, is Jonathan Edwards, *The Works*

of Jonathan Edwards, 2: Religious Affections, edited by John E. Smith (New Haven, 1959).

As important as pietism and Puritanism were to the revivals of colonial North America, these religious awakenings themselves became crucial to evangelical piety and self-understanding. As such the Great Awakenings of the eighteenth and nineteenth centuries are fruitful areas for understanding born-again Protestantism's origins and development. For an insightful collection of essays on this subject, see *Modern Christian Revivals*, edited by Edith L. Blumhofer and Randall Balmer (Urbana, Ill., 1993). Other important guides to the First Great Awakening are Marilyn J. Westerkamp, *Triumph of the Laity: Scots-Irish Piety and The Great Awakening, 1625–1760* (New York, 1988), and Michael J. Crawford, *Seasons of Grace: Colonial New England's Revival Tradition in Its British Context* (New York, 1991). The lives of leading eighteenth-century revivalists are also worthwhile resources on the First Great Awakening. In this case, books on George Whitefield and Jonathan Edwards, such as *Jonathan Edwards and the American Experience*, edited by Nathan O. Hatch and Harry S. Stout (New York, 1988), and Harry S. Stout, *The Divine Dramatist: George Whitefield and the Rise of Modern Evangelicalism* (Grand Rapids, 1991), make outstanding contributions to understanding the complexity of evangelicalism at its origins.

The so-called Second Great Awakening of antebellum America not only built upon but intensified impulses unleashed in the eighteenth century. Although it extends beyond the nineteenth century, William G. McLoughlin, Jr.'s *Modern Revivalism: Charles Grandison Finney to Billy Graham* (New York, 1959) is remarkably astute in its interpretation of revivalism's importance while providing a compelling narrative of nineteenth-century evangelicalism. Another important book on Finney, the leading revivalist of the Second Great Awakening, is Charles E. Hambrick-Stowe, *Charles G. Finney and the Spirit of American Evangelicalism* (Grand Rapids, 1996). Two other important historical works that reveal how evangelicalism became the default position of American Protestantism are Nathan O. Hatch, *The De-*

mocratization of American Christianity (New Haven, 1989), and Christine Leigh Heyrman, *Southern Cross: The Beginnings of the Bible Belt* (New York, 1997). The literature on evangelicalism's influence upon nineteenth-century American society and politics is large and growing. For a sampling of these studies, see Timothy L. Smith, *Revivalism and Social Reform: American Protestantism on the Eve of the Civil War*, rev. ed. (Baltimore, 1980); Charles I. Foster, *An Errand of Mercy: The Evangelical United Front, 1790–1837* (Chapel Hill, 1960); Richard J. Carwardine, *Evangelicals and Politics in Antebellum America* (New Haven, 1993); and Anne C. Loveland, *Southern Evangelicals and the Social Order, 1800–1860* (Baton Rouge, 1980).

Evangelicalism in the period from 1870 to 1920 is not as well known as in other eras. This is partly the result of a religious movement that was pervasive in the established institutions of American culture and society. Windows into evangelical life during this time again come from biographies of important evangelists. Here James R. Findlay, *Dwight L. Moody, American Evangelist: 1838–1899* (Chicago, 1969), and Lyle Dorsett, *Billy Sunday and the Redemption of Urban America* (Grand Rapids, 1991), offer informative accounts of the two greatest exponents of urban revivalism. Douglas Frank, *Less Than Conquerors: How Evangelicals Entered the Twentieth Century* (Grand Rapids, 1986), is a spirited critique, informed by sound historical insights, of evangelical piety during the final decades of the nineteenth century. On the intellectual challenges to evangelical faith posed by Darwinism and biblical criticism, James R. Moore, *The Post-Darwinian Controversies: A Study in the Protestant Struggle to Come to Terms with Darwin in Great Britain and America, 1870–1900* (New York, 1979), and James Turner, *Without God, Without Creed: The Origins of Unbelief in America* (Baltimore, 1985), are necessary reading. Although examining different social settings, Ted Ownby, *Subduing Satan: Religion, Recreation, and Manhood in the Rural South* (Chapel Hill, 1990), and Robert M. Crunden, *Ministers of Reform: The Progressives' Achievement in American Civilization, 1889–1920* (New York, 1982), flesh out aspects of evangelical zeal in the ordinary lives of Americans. Fereno Morton Szasz, *The Divided Mind of Protestant America, 1880–1930* (Tuscaloosa, Ala., 1982), examines the emergence of liberal and conservative wings within the churches upon which evangelicalism had the greatest influence.

INTRODUCTIONS TO TWENTIETH-CENTURY EVANGELICALISM

General introductions to or surveys of evangelical developments in the twentieth century are not as common as focused monographs. Even so, collections of essays provide useful guides to recent evangelical history. Here readers should consult *The Evangelicals: What They Believe, Who They Are, Where They are Changing*, edited by David F. Wells and John D. Woodbridge (Nashville, 1975); *Evangelicalism and Modern America*, edited by George M. Marsden (Grand Rapids, 1984); and *Christian Faith & Practice in the Modern World: Theology from an Evangelical Point of View*, edited by Mark A. Noll and David F. Wells (Grand Rapids, 1988). The recent work of sociologists of religion has added greatly to the understanding of evangelicalism. Christian Smith's two books, *American Evangelicalism: Embattled and Thriving* (Chicago, 1998), and *Christian America? What Evangelicals Really Want* (Berkeley, 2000), along with two by James Davison Hunter, *American Evangelicalism: Conservative Religion and the Quandary of Modernity* (New Brunswick, N.J., 1983), and *Evangelicalism: The Coming Generation* (Chicago, 1987), are worthwhile examples.

One of the more noteworthy aspects of twentieth-century evangelicalism that has not been integrated into the history of the movement is the remarkable growth of Pentecostalism. Early assessments that remain valuable introductions are Vinson Synan, *The Holiness-Pentecostal Movement in the United States* (Grand Rapids, 1971), and Robert Mapes Anderson, *Vision of the Disinherited: The Making of American Pentecostalism* (New York, 1979). David Edwin Harrell, *All Things Are Possible: The Healing and Charismatic Revivals in Modern America* (Bloomington, Ind.,

1975), is perhaps the classic study of Pentecostal influences beyond the official Pentecostal denominations, while Edith W. Blumhofer, *Restoring the Faith: The Assemblies of God, Pentecostalism, and American Culture* (Urbana, Ill., 1993), examines the largest Pentecostal denomination in the United States.

THE FUNDAMENTALIST CONTROVERSY

Older accounts of fundamentalism stressed its rural, Southern, and anti-intellectual tendencies. Norman Furniss, *The Fundamentalist Controversy, 1918–1931* (New Haven, 1954); Ray Ginger, *Six Days or Forever? Tennessee v. John Thomas Scopes* (Chicago, 1968); and Richard Hofstadter, *Anti-Intellectualism in American Life* (New York, 1962), particularly created this impression. Studies since 1960 have treated fundamentalism more sympathetically. Paul A. Carter, "The Fundamentalist Defense of the Faith," in *Change and Continuity in Twentieth-Century America: The 1920s*, edited by John Braeman, Robert Bremmer, and David Brody (Columbus, Ohio, 1968), 179–214; Ernest R. Sandeen, *The Roots of Fundamentalism: British and American Millenarianism*, 1800–1930 (Chicago, 1970); and George M. Marsden, *Fundamentalism and American Culture: The Shaping of Twentieth-Century Evangelicalism, 1870–1925* (New York, 1980), deserve much credit for advancing the study of fundamentalism beyond caricature. Biographical studies of prominent fundamentalists have also helped to rehabilitate fundamentalists' reputation. Here readers should consult C. Allyn Russell, *Voices of American Fundamentalism: Seven Biographical Studies* (Philadelphia, 1976); Lawrence W. Levine, *Defender of the Faith: William Jennings Bryan: The Last Decade, 1915–1925* (Cambridge, Mass., 1987); William Vance Trollinger, Jr., *God's Empire: William Bell Riley and Midwestern Fundamentalism* (Madison, Wisc., 1990); Bradley J. Longfield, *The Presbyterian Controversy: Fundamentalists, Modernists, and Moderates* (New York, 1991); and D. G. Hart, *Defending the Faith: J. Gresham Machen and the Crisis of Conservative Protestantism in Modern America* (Baltimore, 1994). *Controversy in the Twenties: Fundamentalism, Modernism, and Evolution*, edited by Willard B. Gatewood, Jr. (Nashville, 1969), is an excellent anthology of writings by conservative Protestants and their antagonists. The Scopes Trial has taken on mythological status in American history, but Edward J. Larson, *Summer for the Gods: The Scopes Trial and America's Continuing Debate over Science and Religion* (New York, 1997), debunks the hype in a readable and intelligent manner.

Some historians believe the recent controversy in the Southern Baptist Convention is a replaying of the fundamentalist controversy. Because of the SBC's size (approximately fifteen million members), the disputes between so-called conservatives and moderates have generated a wealth of material within the denomination but not much from non-Southern Baptists. For some of this literature, see Nancy Tatom Ammerman, *Baptist Battles: Social Change and Religious Conflict in the Southern Baptist Convention* (New Brunswick, N.J., 1995); *Going for the Jugular: A Documentary History of the SBC Holy War*, edited by Walter B. Shurden and Randy Shepley (Macon, Ga., 1996); David T. Morgan, *The New Crusades, The New Holy Land: Conflict in the Southern Baptist Convention, 1969–1991* (Tuscaloosa, Ala., 1996); James C. Hefley, *The Conservative Resurgence in the Southern Baptist Convention* (Hannibal, Mo., 1991); Paul Pressler, *A Hill on which to Die: One Southern Baptist's Journey* (Nashville, 1999); Bill J. Leonard, *God's Last & Only Hope: The Fragmentation of the Southern Baptist Convention* (Grand Rapids, 1990); and Barry Hankins, *Uneasy in Zion: Southern Baptist Conservatives and American Culture* (Tuscaloosa, Ala., 2002).

EVANGELICALS AND THE BIBLE

Evangelicals' high regard for the Bible receives important consideration in a number of valuable books. *The Bible in America: Essays in Cultural History*, edited by Nathan O. Hatch and Mark A. Noll (New York, 1982), provides a useful introduction to the Bible's function as a cultural icon in the United States and ex-

plains how evangelicalism has contributed to the book's importance. Paul C. Gutjahr, *An American Bible: A History of the Good
Book in the United States, 1777–1880* (Stanford, 1999), and Peter J.
Thuesen, *In Discordance with the Scriptures: American Protestant
Battles over Translating the Bible* (New York, 1999), provide fasci-
nating accounts of how Americans' reverence for the Bible, with
evangelicals leading the way, has turned Scripture into a publishing bonanza.

Dispensationalism dominated evangelical interpretation of the
Bible throughout most of the twentieth century. C. Norman
Kraus, *Dispensationalism in America: Its Rise and Development*
(Richmond, Va., 1958); Timothy P. Weber, *Living in the Shadow
of the Second Coming: American Premillennialism 1875–1925* (New
York, 1979); and Paul Boyer, *When Time Shall Be No More:
Prophecy Belief in Modern American Culture* (Cambridge, Mass.,
1992), cover the topic sympathetically without hiding its bizarre
aspects. Bible colleges and institutes were crucial to the popularity of dispensationalism, and these institutions receive sustained
attention in Virginia Lieson Brereton, *Training God's Army: The
American Bible School, 1880–1940* (Bloomington, Ind., 1990). One
of the side effects of dispensationalism was vigorous foreign missionary activity, a subject explored with care in *Earthen Vessels:
American Evangelicals and Foreign Missions, 1880–1980*, edited by
Joel A. Carpenter and Wilbert R. Shenk (Grand Rapids, 1990).

Creationism is another interpretive grid through which evangelicals have read the Bible. Ronald L. Numbers, *The Creationists: The Evolution of Scientific Creationism* (New York, 1992),
thoroughly documents the contours of evangelical attempts to
read the Bible scientifically, while *Evangelicals and Science in Historical Perspective*, edited by David N. Livingstone, D. G. Hart,
and Mark A. Noll (New York, 1999), explores a wider set of influences on evangelical beliefs about creation. Evangelical understanding of the Bible has also been bound up with inerrancy, a
doctrine that according to some derives from an overly scientific
(read: literal) approach to ancient texts. Some of the best contributions to these discussions are Robert K. Johnston, *Evangelicals*

at an Impasse: Biblical Authority in Practice (Atlanta, 1979); Jack B. Rogers and Donald L. McKim, *The Authority and Interpretation of the Bible: An Historical Approach* (San Francisco, 1979); and John D. Woodbridge, *Biblical Authority: A Critique of the Rogers/McKim Proposal* (Grand Rapids, 1982).

The Bible has not only been a source for knowledge about creation and the day of judgment but also for Christian living. Several books explore evangelical efforts to live by the book they regard as divine: Nancy Tatom Ammerman, *Bible Believers: Fundamentalists in the Modern World* (New Brunswick, N.J., 1987); David Harrington Watt, *A Transforming Faith: Explorations of Twentieth-Century American Evangelicalism* (New Brunswick, N.J., 1991), and *Bible Carrying Christians: Conservative Protestants and Social Power* (New York, 2002). For evangelicals throughout most of the twentieth century, the Bible had specific things to say to women about their domestic responsibilities. Margaret Lamberts Bendroth, *Fundamentalism and Gender, 1875 to the Present* (New Haven, 1993), and Betty A. DeBerg, *Ungodly Women: Gender and the First Wave of American Fundamentalism* (Minneapolis, 1990), provide a good orientation to these views.

NEO-EVANGELICALISM

In the 1940s some fundamentalists believed that belligerency was costing them a hearing in America, so they established a variety of institutions to rehabilitate their mission. Because they used the word "evangelical," their movement was greatly responsible for narrowing the use of this term to conservative Protestants. A book on which I have relied for the middle decades of the twentieth century, which is also the best book on neo-evangelicalism, Joel A. Carpenter, *Revive Us Again: The Reawakening of American Fundamentalism* (New York, 1997), describes how neo-evangelicalism emerged from a fundamentalist subculture and erected a platform for national influence. Carpenter's book, along with Marsden's *Fundamentalism and American Culture*, is

essential reading for the study of twentieth-century evangelicalism. Jon R. Stone, *On the Boundaries of American Evangelicalism:
The Postwar Evangelical Coalition* (New York, 1997), discusses
how neo-evangelicals benefited from the fundamentalist subculture to carve out a distinct identity for evangelicals. For an idea
of what life was like in the evangelical subculture, Shirley Nelson's novel *The Last Year of the War* (New York, 1979) is a
wonderful source. Carl Henry's *The Uneasy Conscience of
Modern Fundamentalism* (Grand Rapids, 1947) alerted fundamentalists to the need to leave their religious ghetto and join the
neo-evangelical movement. Henry was a professor then at Fuller
Seminary, an important institution in the revitalization of mid-
twentieth-century evangelicalism. George M. Marsden, *Reforming Fundamentalism: Fuller Seminary and the New Evangelicalism*
(Grand Rapids, 1986), describes well this school's contribution to
the larger movement. Another professor at Fuller, who eventually became its president, is the subject of another valuable book
on the neo-evangelical movement, Rudolph Nelson, *The Making
and Unmaking of an Evangelical Mind: The Case of Edward Carnell*
(New York, 1987). A guide to understanding the changes in
American religion that evangelicals contributed to and benefited
from is Robert Wuthnow, *The Restructuring of American Religion: Society and Faith Since World War II* (Princeton, 1988).

Billy Graham is a crucial figure in twentieth-century evangelical history in his own right, but he emerged from the networks
established by neo-evangelicalism. The best biography of Graham is William Martin, *A Prophet with Honor: The Billy Graham
Story* (New York, 1991). For Graham's own estimate of his life
and work, see Billy Graham, *Just as I Am: The Autobiography*
(New York, 1997).

EVANGELICAL INTELLECTUAL LIFE

The resurgence of evangelicalism at mid-century through the
fundamentalists who commandeered the word "evangelical"
prompted not only a proliferation of new institutions but a

greater interest in scholarly pursuits. Because Fuller Seminary
was an important expression of this interest, Marsden's *Reforming Fundamentalism* and Nelson's *Making and Unmaking of an
Evangelical Mind* (cited above) are necessary pieces of the evangelical scholarly puzzle. Theological seminaries more generally
were important sites for evangelical academic life, and their significance is one of the themes in *Theological Education in the
Evangelical Tradition*, edited by D. G. Hart and R. Albert Mohler
(Grand Rapids, 1996). The Evangelical Theological Society
(ETS) was another important agency in the scholarly output of
evangelicals. Mark A. Noll's *Between Faith and Criticism: Evangelical Scholarship and the Bible in America* (San Francisco, 1986)
is a history of evangelical biblical scholarship that centers on
ETS. The American Scientific Affiliation is one of the subjects
that Numbers, *The Creationists* (cited above) treats judiciously.
History and the Christian Historian, edited by Ronald A. Wells
(Grand Rapids, 1998), examines evangelical contributions to his-
torical scholarship, especially as cultivated by the Conference on
Faith and History. For signs of evangelical self awareness in the
academy, along with arguments on behalf of Christian scholars,
see Mark A. Noll, *The Scandal of the Evangelical Mind* (Grand
Rapids, 1994), and George M. Marsden, *The Outrageous Idea of
Christian Scholarship* (New York, 1997). The influence of Francis
A. Schaeffer has not attracted the sustained study it deserves, but
Ronald W. Ruegsegger, *Reflections on Francis Schaeffer* (Grand
Rapids, 1986), is a preliminary effort.

EVANGELICAL POLITICS

Without the mobilization of evangelicals in the 1980 presidential
election that sent Ronald Reagan to the White House, the study
of evangelicalism might be where it was three decades ago—
largely dormant. But because politics involves power, and because Americans are generally suspicious of mixing religion and
power, the study of evangelicals and American politics has paved
the way for the study of born-again Protestants. Before the reli-

gious right attracted the attention of journalists and political strategists, fundamentalists made their own contribution to American politics. Leo Ribuffo, *The Old Christian Right: The Protestant Far Right from the Great Depression to the Cold War* (Philadelphia, 1983), offers a candid assessment of fundamentalist politics that is equally tough on evangelicals and mainstream politicians. Biographies provide another fruitful approach to fundamentalist politics; here Glen Jeansonne, *Gerald L. K. Smith: Minister of Hate* (Baton Rouge, 1997) is profitable.

Historians and social scientists have devoted their attention mainly to recent evangelical involvement in American politics. The rise of the religious right has generated important work from sociologists and political scientists. The following are useful resources: Michael Lienesch, *Redeeming America: Piety and Politics in the New Christian Right* (Chapel Hill, 1993); Steve Bruce, *The Rise and Fall of the New Christian Right: Conservative Protestant Politics in America, 1978–1988* (New York, 1988); William C. Martin, *With God on Our Side: The Rise of the Religious Right in America* (New York, 1996); Clyde Wilcox, *God's Warriors? The Christian Right in Twentieth-Century America* (Baltimore, 1992); John Green et al., *Religion and the Culture Wars: Dispatches from the Front* (Lanham, Md., 1996); and James Davison Hunter, *Culture Wars: The Struggle to Define America* (New York, 1991). I benefited greatly from Lisa McGirr, *The Origins of the New American Right* (Princeton, 2001), especially her examination of southern California evangelicals.

Evangelicals themselves have also reflected carefully on their political involvements while offering advice to their fellow citizens about better and worse ways to order American society. The following works give some access to evangelicals' reflections in their own voice: Paul B. Henry, *Politics for Evangelicals* (Valley Forge, Pa., 1974); Mark Hatfield, *Between a Rock and a Hard Place* (Waco, Tex., 1976); Francis A. Schaeffer, *A Christian Manifesto* (Westchester, Ill., 1981); *Piety and Politics: Evangelicals and Fundamentalists Confront the World*, edited by Richard John Neuhaus and Michael Cromartie (Washington, D.C., 1987);

Being Christian Today: An American Conversation, edited by Richard John Neuhaus and George Weigel (Washington, D.C., 1991); Don E. Eberly, *Restoring the Good Society: A New Vision for Politics and Culture* (Grand Rapids, 1994); Mark A. Noll, *One Nation Under God? Christian Faith and Political Action in America* (New York, 1988); and Lawrence E. Adams, *Going Public: Christian Responsibility in a Divided America* (Grand Rapids, 2002).

EVANGELICALS AND POPULAR CULTURE

The tendency in studies of evangelicalism has been to concentrate on theology because of the doctrinal conflicts that dominated the fundamentalist controversy. The rise of the religious right has also made the theme of politics a close second to theology. The subject of evangelical attitudes to and their production of culture has generally finished last in the race of academic interest. Still, a number of studies provide helpful points of entry for further analysis.

The historical material is still thin. Carpenter's *Revive Us Again* (cited above) examines carefully the religious subculture of evangelicalism just after the fundamentalist controversy. Douglas Carl Abrams, *Selling the Old-Time Religion: American Fundamentalists and Mass Culture* (Athens, Ga., 2001), explores how fundamentalists used media outlets and entertainment techniques to promote their faith. Paul Apostolidis, *Stations of the Cross: Adorno and the Christian Right* (Durham, N.C., 2000), explores the connections between Christian radio and conservative politics. A critical examination of televangelists can be found in Janice Peck, *The Crisis of Meaning and the Appeal of Religious Television* (Cresskill, N.J., 1993).

For recent discussions either by or about evangelicals and contemporary popular culture, the following books are valuable: *Evangelicals and the Mass Media*, edited by Quentin J. Schultze (Grand Rapids, 1990); Kenneth A. Myers, *All God's Children and Blue Suede Shoes: Christians and Popular Culture* (Westchester, Ill., 1989); Quentin J. Schultze, et al., *Dancing in the Dark: Youth, Pop-*

ular Culture, and the Electronic Media (Grand Rapids, 1991); and William D. Romanowski, *Eyes Wide Open: Looking for God in Popular Culture* (Grand Rapids, 2001), and *Pop Culture Wars: Religion and the Role of Entertainment in American Life* (Downers Grove, Ill., 1996). Important for understanding the popularity of fiction written by evangelicals about the second coming of Christ is Jan Blodgett, *Protestant Evangelical Literary Culture and Contemporary Society* (Westport, Conn., 1997), and Boyer, *When Time Shall Be No More* (cited above).

The evangelical churches that make the most use of popular culture and contemporary music in their worship are the so-called megachurches and those connected to the charismatic movement. These congregations come in for careful analysis in Donald E. Miller, *Reinventing American Protestantism: Christianity in the New Millennium* (Berkeley, 1997); Kimon Howland Sargeant, *Seeker Churches: Promoting Traditional Religion in a Nontraditional Way* (New Brunswick, N.J., 2001) and Mark A. Shibley, *Resurgent Evangelicalism in the United States: Mapping Cultural Change Since 1970* (Columbia, S.C., 1996).

Although this overview represents only a small portion of the scholarly literature on (and in some cases by) evangelicals, many aspects of born-again Protestantism remain to be studied. Perhaps one of the greatest needs is whether the label "evangelical" is sufficiently durable to contain all those Protestants who are outside or are ambivalent about the oldest and largest denominations in the United States. A book that examines the limitations of evangelicalism as a classification of American Christianity is D. G. Hart, *The Lost Soul of American Protestantism* (Lanham, Md., 2002).

Index

A NOTE ON THE AUTHOR

D. G. Hart was born in Abington, Pennsylvania, and studied at Temple University, Westminster Seminary, Harvard University, and Johns Hopkins University, where he received a Ph.D. in American history. He has written widely on religion in American history, including *Defending the Faith*, *The University Gets Religion*, and *The Lost Soul of American Protestantism*, and has co-edited *Evangelicals and Science in Historical Perspective*, *New Directions in American Religious History*, and *Religious Advocacy and the Writing of American History*. He is at present academic dean and professor of church history at Westminster Theological Seminary in California.